THE BEACHLEY BOYS

BY

BRIAN ELKS

A Sin to Tell a Lie

THE BEACHLEY BOYS

Or

'IT'S A SIN TO TELL A LIE'

PUBLISHED IN 2007 BY BRIAN A F ELKS
12, CHESHIRE RD
THAME, OXON
Tel 01844 214361

ALL RIGHTS RESERVED

Printed and bound by CPI Antony Rowe, Eastbourne

ISBN 978-0-9555073-1-1

© **Brian A F Elks**

A Sin to Tell a Lie

DEDICATION

FOR THOSE WHO WISH TO REMEMBER
FOR THOSE WHO CANNOT FORGET
FOR THOSE WHO LIVE ON IN OUR MEMORIES.

*'Teach us delight in simple things
and mirth that seeks no bitter springs;
forgiveness free of evil done
and love to all men 'neath the sun.'*

(from the Apprentices Passing Out Church Service)

Other Books by the Author

Light a Candle   An Uncivil War
My Heart and I   Come Back, Dinky Bumstead
May the Bluebells Bloom   A Grandfather's Tale
Give Me the Child

A Sin to Tell a Lie

ARMY APPRENTICES SCHOOL

THE BEACHLEY BOYS

*'We were called boys, after the term 'boy soldier'; we
referred to ourselves as boys
And I believe to our dying day we will think of
ourselves as boys.*

*But that is our strength, we do not wish to grow old
So in our minds we will always be young
There is always so much to achieve tomorrow
That we cannot afford to grow old.'*

A Sin to Tell a Lie

THE BEACHLEY BOYS

CONTENTS

Foreword

Heavenly Stocking Tops

Memorabilia & Mementoes
    Historical Note; Army Apprentices School in the 1950's
    Beachley Camp map, Attestation Form
    Beachley Humour, Postcards Home, Beachley Pin-ups
    A Beachley Christmas Card. The Christmas Menu, 1951,
    Et al

Captain Marsden's Carafe

Goodbye-e-e-e!

Mementoes & Memorabilia
    50B Passing Out Service, Apprenticeship Papers &
    Education Certificates, Roll Calls - 50A & 50B,
    Passing Out Programme, etc

Acknowledgement

Some Poetry   - 'Old Friends Passing By'
                     'The Last Beachley Boy'

Afterwards

Space for personal notes

Foreword

THE ARMY APPRENTICES SCHOOL (LATER COLLEGE) AT BEACHLEY CAMP, NEAR CHEPSTOW, WAS OPEN FOR 70 YEARS, FROM 1924 UNTIL IT CLOSED IN 1994. THOUSANDS OF BOYS FROM ALL OVER THE COUNTRY STARTED AT AROUND THE AGE 15 to 16 ON A THREE YEAR APPRENTICESHIP BEFORE JOINING THE ROYAL ENGINEERS, REME OR ROYAL ORDNANCE CORPS, etc. THEY ALWAYS CALLED THEMSELVES THE 'BEACHLEY BOYS'. ALTHOUGH ESSENTIALLY AN ARMY TECHNICAL TRAINING CENTRE, MANY A LAD BLANCHED WHEN FACED WITH AN UNEXPECTED BUT ESSENTIAL EDUCATION

SYSTEM. THERE WAS NO FUTURE IN THE ARMY FOR IDLENESS OR ILLITERACY!

EACH PASSING YEAR SEVERAL HUNDRED MEN STILL GATHER TOGETHER AT CHEPSTOW WITH A SENSE OF PRIDE AND COMRADESHIP IN MEMORY OF THEIR YOUTHFUL YEARS TOGETHER AND, VERY OFTEN, SO MANY LATER YEARS OF SERVICE TOGETHER AS FRIENDS IN THE ARMY.

THE PURPOSE OF THIS STORY IS TO PROVOKE MEMORIES, LAUGHTER AND PERHAPS SOME NOSTALGIA FOR A BYGONE AGE. SURELY WE HAVE THE RIGHT TO WONDER HOW WE WILL BE REPLACED BECAUSE WE FITTED INTO SOCIETY AND THE ARMY SO COMFORTABLY AND EFFICIENTLY BECAUSE WE WERE PROFESSIONALS. THAT IS NO LIE, NOR A SIN TO SAY IT—BUT ONCE WE WERE BOYS.

A SIN TO TELL A LIE

**'BE SURE IT'S TRUE WHEN YOU SAY I LOVE YOU
IT'S A SIN TO TELL A LIE
MILLIONS OF HEARTS HAVE BEEN BROKEN
JUST BECAUSE THESE WORDS WERE SPOKEN
I LOVE YOU, I LOVE YOU - I LOVE YOU
IF YOU BREAK MY HEART I'LL SURELY DIE
SO BE SURE THAT IT'S TRUE WHEN YOU SAY I LOVE YOU
BECAUSE IT'S A SIN – A DOGGONE SIN, TO TELL A LIE!'**

A Sin to Tell a Lie

HEAVENLY STOCKING TOPS

September 2006

How could the years have passed so quickly? I gazed through the old gates that have been retained as a memento, down the avenue of trees and into the camp; a changed camp as I could see but then it was 49 years since I had left here for the second time when the 'electronic' trades were sent to Arborfield.

My friend Brian Woolsey, a long ago Beachley comrade, asked me to face the camera and I did so reluctantly, unwilling to turn my back on my memories for a moment. We had travelled over a hundred miles to meet with old friends at the BOBA Reunion; they were waiting at the hotel in Chepstow. But there were others here with us this day. They had not grown old. What held me was the vision in my mind's eye as large numbers of long forgotten faces marched down the avenue and left wheeled towards the Gymnasium. Someone had said that it had been demolished but I could still see it.

"Face the camera! – right – now you take mine" The camera was one of those sophisticated modern 'digitals'. This was not going to be easy! It must have cost more than our entire three years pay when we joined as boys in 1950.

We had last walked out through these gates together in late August 1953 having completed our 3 years training. The future beckoned enticingly, we could not wait a moment longer to go out into the world. He was destined for the RE. I was off to the

A Sin to Tell a Lie

REME. Little did we realise that over 50 years would pass by with a dizzying speed, leaving us with life's baggage, troubled joints and diminished eyesight before we met again.

I walked back towards the 'Gates' in silence; they were still there, all those ghosts of the past. Those boys I remembered had not gone. No matter that it was the home of a modern infantry battalion; they could not march with greater pride or with more precision than we had. I could see and hear the lads as plain as when my eyes and ears were still young – and the band playing. My eyes suddenly went moist.

'A British soldier- ta da da darr dum, ta da da darr-dum- da, da, dar -dum- dum- dum- dum……..'

My friend broke into my reverie, "Can you feel it, mate? - they are all around us. My skin is tingling and…. There goes Taffy..and Ted…and….."

He stopped and I nodded, unable to speak; as if it would break a spell. We must have stood there a good many minutes, just watching in silence. Each lost in thought whilst our youth paraded before our eyes and boyish figures greeted us. I also recalled coming back through these gates in 1956 and the feeling of disappointment then. The real army was somewhere else. Let someone else teach the lads. Only years later did I realise and accept it was in fact a privilege given to very few.

At last my friend spoke, "Do you remember when we cleared all the stones from that field to make it suitable to play football?" Of course I remembered, evenings of work filling buckets. 'Do you remember?' was to become a frequent question later as we reminisced at the bar.

From the gate we went to the cricket field and the cinder track that had graced the area near to the site of the old Sergeants Mess and the water tower, buildings that had long gone. In our time here we had spent hours and hours in this place, training

and competing; perhaps it is the vanity of age but I do recall we rarely lost! Within that old Sergeants Mess in May 1957 I had prepared for the most severe examination of my life; burning the midnight oil. Such a pity that the first Severn Bridge passes overhead but that is progress I suppose. As we drove away and passed by the old entrance gate the ghosts of apprentices waved a farewell. Further down the road my friend asked if we could go in (there was a new entrance). We were made welcome and allowed to drive around the camp. Enough remains of the old ground layout to make the place familiar. When leaving we stopped to say thank you. It was only then that we realised that the discreet guard holding an automatic rifle was in fact a very desirable and lovely young lady.

"Blimey, they never made'em like that when we were lads here," said my friend.

I agreed. It was quite irrational really but I wondered if she ever wore proper stockings; the ones that stop somewhere in the vicinity of heaven. We had responded to our hormonal growth by pursuing the girls in nearby Chepstow. "Do you remember our last evening here in 53? - we caught the bus into Chep. Lovely evening I recall."

"Yeah, that's right," he replied, "you were going to meet – Margery, was that it? Was that what she was called? And I was going to meet – what was her name?" He frowned. Oh dear I thought, perhaps our memories are going too! "Whatever happened to you two?" he asked.

"She sent me a 'dear john' when we had been separated for three weeks – but it was inevitable."

"You were lucky, mine came with the next day's post!"

Late August, 1953

We had chosen this spot high over the River Wye, it gave the maximum seclusion and provided it hadn't rained lately it offered a comfortable grassy spot to lie down safe from prying eyes. Our meetings, two or three times a week, had become almost a ritual. Inclement weather directed us to the back stall of the Chepstow cinema where we embraced as ardently as other patrons allowed; though his had been a gradual process of discovery and growing familiarity. Luckily for us the films changed at least twice weekly, not that we really watched but it made an excuse to go. When Winter turned to Spring and then

CHEPSTOW CASTLE ABD BRIDGE

Summer we had looked around for a secluded spot. Most of the town was already occupied by courting lads and lassies so we gravitated to the hillside on the other side of the river, overlooking the castle. There was one other great advantage, it was minutes from a bus stop and ensured she always caught the last bus home.

  As we walked up the hill the sun shone, it was really a lovely warm day but I only had eyes for her. She didn't smile readily but when she did I was bowled over, she was the first girl I had ever really liked. There was of course the icing on the cake. She looked very much like Audrey Hepburn and I had stolen her without a qualm from a good friend over six months ago. Nothing was said about it but we both knew I was leaving in the morning to join my new unit in Kent. Much too far for any casual visit and expensive enough, other than with a warrant, to deter travel on my weekly pay. None of this was spoken about but for our last two meetings we had clung to each other as if some terrible event was unfolding. Tomorrow was never mentioned until that very last moment when the last bus stopped and I whispered that I would write as soon as possible as we embraced; then she got on the bus without looking back.

Our little spot was unoccupied, not that I expected otherwise, so in true gentlemanly fashion I put my jacket on the ground for us to lie on.
My lips nibbled at the top of a tantalising breast but the brassiere remained firmly in place, although probing fingers somehow found a delightful but elusive nipple; that made her shudder and my finger tingle. I fervently hoped that her shudder was delight but although she gave a gentle moan I couldn't bring myself to ask in case the spell was broken. My hand went to her knee and gently caressed while slowly moving upwards, Oh God, there was something totally wonderful about the soft skin at the top of a stocking. Before tonight the hand would have been pushed back several times but not tonight. As my hand caressed her thigh her legs opened a fraction and she clung fiercely to me. I thought my poor cock was going to burst out of my trousers; surely a seam would break under the strain. Almost unable to breathe, my finger felt a moist panty, the edge lifted and I was in heaven and her hips convulsed to my touch. Then she did something she had never done before and had never been done to me before. Her hand stretched over and felt for my cock. Moments later she loosened my belt and felt inside. I do not remember how long we lay like that but it was quite wonderful as we climaxed together several times. She clung hard to me and every now and then she would whisper between kisses, 'I love you - I love you."
'I love you too- I really, really do."

A Sin to Tell a Lie

But one day we reach September -

'When we were young lads acourting the girls
We played us a waiting game
If the girls refused with a toss of their curls
We'd let the old world take a number of twirls
Then we'd ply them with tender and rapturous words
And as time came around they came our way
As time come around they came.

But it's a long, long time from May to December
And the days grow short when you reach September
When the autumn weather turns the leaves to flame
One hasn't got time for the waiting game
Oh the days dwindle down - to a precious few
    September ----- November
So these few precious days I'll spend with you
These golden days I'll spend with you....'

A Sin to Tell a Lie

ARMY APPRENTICES SCHOOL

A PROUD CAREER

A Sin to Tell a Lie

ARMY APPRENTICES SCHOOLS

The Importance of Apprentice Tradesmen to the Modern Army

INTENSIVE development of mechanisation has taken place in the Army in recent years. As a result of this the need for highly skilled men in all the various trades and arms has grown enormously. To fill this need, the system of Army apprentice tradesmen, which was well established even before the recent war, is undergoing rapid development and expansion.

This booklet is designed to give an insight into the work of Army Apprentices Schools, where apprentice tradesmen are trained. Nearly a quarter of a century has gone by since the system of Army technical schools for boys was started. During that time the schools have trained many thousands of fine craftsmen in a great number of trades, some of which are listed at the end of this booklet. These men, taking their places with the Colours, have shown conclusively that their knowledge and training have fitted them to play a valuable and indeed indispensable part in the modern Army.

The Army of to-day is highly progressive. It is provided with new weapons, vehicles and equipment of tremendous variety and increased complexity. The effective use of all these demands an even higher achievement in the training of technical personnel, and for this reason the Army Apprentices Schools are being improved and developed still more. Not only is the number of schools being increased, but greatly improved facilities are being provided at each of them.

Any parent who is anxious to secure a promising future for his son cannot do better than consider taking advantage of the Army apprenticeship system. By doing so he will obtain for the boy a complete technical training as a skilled tradesman of the highest standard, leading to a really worth-while and interesting career.

Conditions of entry and other details are given in later pages of this booklet, where it will be seen that training at Army Apprentices Schools is given at no cost whatever either to the boy's parents or to the boy himself.

For speedy communication the Army needs expert wireless tradesmen. Here an apprentice is carrying out adjustments to a set.

Some of the Trades for which Boys are Trained

Armourer	Blacksmith	Line Mechanic
Electrician	Sheet Metal Worker	Operator (Wireless and Keyboard)
Fitter	Carpenter and Joiner	Operator (Keyboard and Line)
Instrument Mechanic	Bricklayer and Mason	Operator (Wireless and Line)
Telecommunication Mechanic	Radio Mechanic	
Turner	Telegraph Mechanic	Lineman
Vehicle Mechanic		

LIST OF SCHOOLS

ARMY APPRENTICES SCHOOL
Chepstow, Mon.

*

ARMY APPRENTICES SCHOOL
Arborfield, Berks.

*

ARMY APPRENTICES SCHOOL
Harrogate, Yorks.

A Sin to Tell a Lie

Pay is issued from the day the boy joins the school and is 1s 6d. a day for the first year, 2s. a day for the second year, and 2s 6d. a day for the third year. If the boy reaches the age of 17½ years while still at the school, his pay is automatically increased to 4s. a day. Small increments are also paid to boy N.C.Os. The training at the schools is of course entirely free. Parents are put to no expense from the day the boy is accepted and joins the school.

Leave consists of eight weeks a year: a month in the summer, a fortnight each at Christmas and Easter. Free travel warrants are provided and allowances issued in lieu of rations.

*

APPLICATION FORMS AND FURTHER INFORMATION

The necessary application forms can be obtained from any Army recruiting officer or from the schools themselves.

The commandants of the schools welcome visits at any time from parents of boys already at the school or those considering sending their sons. Such visits should if possible be arranged by letter in advance.

Conditions of entry, service, trades taught, etc., are liable to alteration from time to time, and it is, therefore, desirable to make inquiries for more detailed information.

ARMY RECRUITING OFFICE

Memorabilia & Mementoes

Historical Note; Army Apprentices School, 1950-53

Those who were there need no explanation; for others a few words of explanation may help to understand this book. In the first place the school had several names over the years but it was the Army Apprentices School in the period this story covers.

The staff were mainly experienced soldiers and officers allocated from different regiments and corps. In the training workshops there were additional numbers of civilian instructors. Boys were recruited after examination at about 15 and joined in two batches each year. Although a parent had to sign the enlistment papers each boy was committed to the army until 18 and was further contracted to serve for a minimum of eight years thereafter, plus reserve duty.

The first half-yearly batch arrived in February and the second in September, hence the titles such as 50A (Joined in Feb 1950) and 50B that followed a group as its identity throughout the school period and has always been used to identify ourselves

A Sin to Tell a Lie

COME, OH CHOSEN ONE!

THE WAR OFFICE,
(A.G.10.),
LONDON, S.W.1.

27/Misc/7941/AG10
INDEX No. ..151....

Sir/Madam,

I am directed to inform you that your son/ward attained the necessary standard of qualification in the Army Apprentice Tradesmen en**trance** examination held on 29th June, 1950, and that he has been selected for training as an Apprentice Tradesman at an Army Apprentices School.

Provided he is **still** physically fit and otherwise eligible, his enlistment will be carried out on or about the 5th Sept 1950.

/The

Mr. E. Carwickes

The officer in charge of the recruiting centre at which he sat the examination has been asked to tell you the date, time and place at which he will be required to attend for enlistment.

If for any reason he is unable to accept the vacancy offered, please inform the War Office (A.G.10) immediately, quoting his index number.

I am, Sir/Madam,
Your obedient Servant,

Director of Manpower Planning.

and our allegiance, later in life.

The apprenticeship period was divided into six month blocks or terms and, like all military personnel, uniform was obligatory. For most of my time at Beachley the apprentices wore Service Dress, very similar to the khaki uniform worn by soldiers in the First World War. Boys were initially put into the Headquarters Company for the first six months of basic training and induction. During this time a trade was allocated after exposure to practical work and tests. But before that we were made into soldiers. Blood, sweat, toil and tears! You are soldiers first was the unvarying regulation. After six months the survivors were divided up and allocated to three or four other companies. It was these companies that formed the basis of competition and each company was divided into platoons by intake grouping. Wide ranging competitions from drill to all the major sports were used to promote esprit and there was great pride in being the 'Champion Company'. The only thing not subject to competition was the trade and trade training, except of course at an individual level. Each company was identified by a coloured plastic disc worn behind the cap badge; black for C Company, light blue for D, red for A and green for B. Sometime in 1951 A Company was disbanded but I do not recall anyone explaining why at the time.

There were NCO ranks awarded to Apprentices and a considerable amount of discipline and supervision was undertaken by these NCOs, which included the position of apprentice 'RSM'.

Our kit was almost exactly like that issued to regular army soldiers and we were subject to the same discipline. For the unfortunate there was a Guardroom with cells and the normal punishment system for minor offences of being confined to barracks, known to all the boys as jankers. This consisted of extra parades and many hours of unpaid labour. We attended church every day except on a Saturday. If ever we went to war

A Sin to Tell a Lie

PICK UP THY BED AND EN-TRAIN

Army Form O 1735

REGIMENTAL ROUTE & MOVEMENT ORDER

Authority for move: Rectg. Rgs.
Unit Ref. No.: BRC/12/50.

THE PERSONNEL NAMED ON THIS ORDER WILL PROCEED AS FOLLOWS:—

From (Dispatching Unit):— Army Rectg Centre, 118 Queens Rd. Brighton

To (Receiving Unit):— OC Army Apprentices School, Chepstow, Monmouthshire

On (Date of move):— 7-9-50.

Senior member IC party:— —

Personnel concerned:—

Boy. DURHAM. John Patrick

Movement details (Route, times, etc.):—

Guildford to Waterloo. Change.
Waterloo to Paddington By Underground.
Paddington to Chepstow. Detrain.
Change Newport.

Date: 6.9.50

Signature and rank of Officer Dispatching Unit.

BRIGHTON

it was guaranteed that our accumulated 'brownie points' would ensure our survival. Atheism was most definitely forbidden! (Although I do believe 'C of E Atheist' was permitted provided you still went to church and attended church parades).

It was mandatory to attend general education lessons for three years or until such time as both the 2nd and 1st class Army Education certificates were obtained, these were essential to future promotion. Pay was fairly limited but even that was controlled by restricted allocation during term time. We were forbidden to drink alcohol; which was just as well because we couldn't afford to buy it! We were also forbidden to marry but I never recall that being considered unfair nor unreasonable – I wonder why?

Joining up for most lads was the first big adventure alone out into the world. Alone that is except for the other seven hundred odd lads who all wanted to be in the cookhouse queue before you!

Following the end of WW2 our country endured many lean years and rationing was prevalent. The deepening 'Cold War' demanded a large standing army and 'National Service' prevailed, putting great pressure on both the services and country. Pay levels were comparatively poor. A second hand car would cost several years wages! (In fact at least four to five times the annual pay of an army sergeant) A pipe full of 'Bruno', puffed by strong silent types was the way to a young lady's heart!! The Army suffered because expenditure on equipment was limited and our rifles would not have been out of place in the Boer War. Saturday morning cinema clubs for young children thrived and Butlin's Holiday Camps brimmed with life. I do recall that my greatest ambition at the age of 14 was to own a bicycle with a three speed gear. It was an ambition never fulfilled.

A Sin to Tell a Lie

YOU ARE SPECIALLY CHOSEN

Telephone:- BRIGHTON 25096.   No. 33, Recruiting Centre,
                                  118, Queen's Road, BRIGHTON.
                                  Date.... 25/8/50

Reference 27/Misc/7937/AG10

Sir/Madam,

Army Apprentice Tradesmen Examination held on

___29 JUNE 1950___

1. I have been informed by the War Office that your son/ward has been allotted a vacancy at A.T.School CHEPSTOW and that he may be accepted for enlistment into the Regular Army.

2. If you agree to his enlistment, will you please arrange for him to attend at this recruiting centre on 1st Sept. 50 at 10 am

3. He should bring with him:-
   (a) The enclosed Army Form B 59, completed on the back and signed by you and a Witness to your signature.
   (b) His National Registration Identity Card & Birth Certificate.
   (c) His Ration Book & National Insurance Card (if in Possession)
   (d) His hair brush, tooth brush and comb.
   (e) This letter.
   (f) He will be provided with a soldiers box on joining his School, but it is recommended that he should bring his own padlock (size about 1½ to 2 inches)

4. He will be enlisted for training as an apprentice tradesman and sent to join the Army Apprentice School at CHEPSTOW
on THIRD 7 SEPT 50.
The terms of enlistment will be to serve with the Colours up to the age of 18 years - thereafter for a period of either 8 years with the Colours and 4 years in the Royal Army Reserve, or 12 years with the Colours. He may choose whichever of these two alternatives he prefers.

5. On joining he will be provided with a complete outfit, including uniform, and it will only be necessary to take with him the clothing and necessaries (including those shown in para 3 (d) above, that are likely to be required for his journey.

6. If he does not wish to accept the vacancy now offered, please return this letter immediately to me, with your remarks.

7. If he wishes to accept the vacancy, but will be unable to attend for enlistment on the date shown in para 2 above, please notify me immediately, giving the reason & a date on which he will be able to attend. No guarantee, however, can be given that this vacancy will be kept open for him.

8. The enclosed Army Form B 59 is returned for you to fill in the answers on the back of the form (consent to enlistment). The answers should be completed in all places where marked X, BOTH PARENTS should sign if possible, if one is unable to sign, the reason should be stated.

9. Railway Warrant, which should be exchanged for a ticket, for his journey enclosed.

                    I am, Sir/Madam,
                    Your obedient Servant,
                         M Willm
                    O.C. No.33 Recruiting Centre.   Major.

To:- PARENTS J.P. DURKAN,
     53. ARDMORE AVE.
     GUILDFORD. SURREY.

A Sin to Tell a Lie

TV was in its infancy and a 9 inch television, which was very unreliable, cost £45 and was beyond the reach of most people. It was a lucky apprentice who owned a radio. A portable record player was so heavy that only an Olympic weight lifter could carry it around for more than five minutes! Smoking was fashionable and manly men and alluring girls advertised and vied for our custom. 1950 saw the end of petrol, paper and soap rationing but other items were still rationed or in very short supply. Sweet rationing existed until 1953. However the situation gradually improved. For our entertainment the cinemas often showed three double feature programmes each week.

The apprentice training scheme seemed to enjoy considerable favour with the army and I do not recall a time during my service when it was thought it might be discontinued. *I had been in the REME for only four days when a Warrant Officer told me I was playing hockey that afternoon. 'I don't play hockey, Q,' I replied. 'Don't be daft,' he said, 'you're an ex-boy from Beachley, aren't you! Get a stick, we bully off at 2pm.' That was my personal introduction to another glorious sport.*

As our career's developed and life seemed to go on as normal, the possibility of the closure of Beachley or the Apprenticeship Scheme never crossed our minds; surely the old school would go on for ever. Even its closure in the 1990's initially went unnoticed by most old boys, including myself. Now we live on memories, the self pride that was instilled in our glory days, and revived comradeship.

A Sin to Tell a Lie

Included within this book there are extracts from the 'ROBOT', the School Magazine, of the period. It did not prove easy to extract data relating to sporting awards. There are omissions, considerable miss-spelling of names and often a lack of initials. Should anyone feel slighted please forgive me. I have left several blank pages so that personal inserts or notes can be added should you wish.

Chepstow Castle and the Castle Walk.

A Sin to Tell a Lie
APPRENTICES CONDITIONS OF ENTRY, 1950

REGULAR ARMY APPRENTICE TRADESMEN ENTRANCE EXAMINATION 29th June, 1950

CONDITIONS OF ENTRY AND TERMS OF SERVICE

GENERAL

1. An entrance examination will be held at centres appointed by certain local education authorities and at army recruiting centres in the United Kingdom and Jersey (Channel Isles) on 29th June, 1950.

   These notes will give you some useful information and if you want fuller details ask your local Army recruiting officer.

VACANCIES

2. Boys may join the Regular Army as the result of this examination as :-

   (a) Class 'A' apprentice tradesmen)
) A list of these is given in para. 9
   (b) Class 'B' apprentice tradesmen)

   (c) Apprentice chefs in Army Catering Corps

ELIGIBILITY

3. Candidates must be :-

   (a) (i) British subjects of European race,

   OR

   (ii) British subjects or British protected persons of non-European race, who are resident in the United Kingdom.

   (b) Within the following age limits on date of joining unit :-

   15 - 16½ years of age in all areas where the school leaving age is 15 years.

   14½ - 16½ years of age where the school leaving age has not yet been raised to 15 years.

   The boy must have properly have left school before he is enlisted.

APPLICATIONS

4. Applications to sit for the examination must reach army recruiting officers by 31st May, 1950. The following certificates should accompany the application :-

   Birth or baptismal certificate

   Certificate of character from not less than two responsible persons

SYLLABUS FOR EXAMININATION

5. The examination will consist of the following subjects :-

	Subject	Time allowed
(a)	MATHEMATICS (Mental Test)	Twenty minutes

A Sin to Tell a Lie
APPRENTICES CONDITIONS OF ENTRY, 1950

Subject	Time allowed

(b) **MATHEMATICS**

(i)	Reductions of money, weights and measures	
(ii)	The metric system	
(iii)	Vulgar fractions	
(iv)	Decimal conversion to and from vulgar fractions	Forty minutes
(v)	Ratio and proportion	
(vi)	Averages	
(vii)	Areas and volume	
(viii)	Simple equations	

(c) **ENGLISH**

(i)	a letter or essay	
(ii)	Questions to test the candidate's knowledge and command of English	One hour

(d) **GENERAL KNOWLEDGE**

Questions on everyday matters including sport, Elementary science, music, books and present day affairs in which candidates are considered likely to be interested.   One hour

(e) A liberal choice of questions is given in (b), (c) and in (d).

ENTRANCE EXAMINATION FEE

6. All candidates competing at the entrance examination, except boys of the Duke of York's Royal Military School and the Queen Victoria's School; will be required to pay an entrance fee of 2s. 6d. This fee will be collected by the supervising officer before the examination starts.

TRAVELLING EXPENSES

7. (a) A refund of travelling expenses connected with the candidate's attendance at medical and educational examinations is permissible in certain circumstances.

   (b) Candidates called in for enlistment will be given single railway warrant's (or bus warrant's), or the actual fare instead, for a journey from their place of residence to the recruiting centre when the total distance exceeds two miles.

SECONDARY SCHOOL OBLIGATIONS

8. Parents of an applicant who is attending a secondary school, who have entered into an agreement with the local education authority regarding the attendance of their son at the school, are respectfully reminded of their obligations. They should consult the education authority and notify their intention to enter the boy as a candidate at the army apprentice tradesmen's entrance examination being held on 29th June, 1950. In many cases local authorities are themselves conducting the examination and may be able to help parents by accepting their application and nominating a boy for the examination.

A Sin to Tell a Lie
APPRENTICES CONDITIONS OF ENTRY, 1950

- 3 -

CORPS AND TRADES OPEN

9. (a) The list of corps open and the trades to be taught are as follows :-

Trades taught	Corps open (indicated with an "X")									
	RAC	RA	RE	R. Sigs	Inf	RASC	RAMC	RAOC	REME	ACC
Class 'A' Apprentice Tradesmen										
Armourer									X	
Blacksmith			X				X		X	
Bricklayer and mason			X				X			
Carpenter and joiner			X						X	
Draughtsman (architectural)			X							
Draughtsman (mechanical)			X							
Electrical fitter		X								
Electrician	X		X				X			
Electrician (vehicle and plant)									X	
Engine fitter			X							
Fitter			X						X	
Fitter (engine room)		X								
Fitter (gun)	X	X								
Instrument mechanic			X						X	
Line mechanic				X						
Operator (keyboard)				X						
Operator (wireless and line)				X						
Painter and decorator			X							
Plumber and pipefitter			X							
Quantity Surveyor's Assistant			X							
Radio mechanic				X						
Sheet metal worker and welder			X						X	
Survey trades			X							
Telecommunications mechanic									X	
Telegraph mechanic				X						
Turner			X						X	
Vehicle mechanic	X	X	X			X		X	X	
Class 'B' Apprentice Tradesmen										
Clerk	X		X	X	X	X	X	X		
Army Catering Corps										
Apprentice chef										X

(b) Selection of trades

For certain trades the number of vacancies is limited. Candidates are advised, therefore, to select four trades from those given above and enter them in order of preference in Section II of the Nomination Form (Army Form B 59). Four corps open in the trades selected should be similarly entered in section II of AF B 59.

(The AF B 59 is a very simple form with which you are not likely to have any difficulty. If you have any doubts about it ask your local Army Recruiting Officer and he will help you).

A Sin to Tell a Lie
APPRENTICES CONDITIONS OF ENTRY, 1950

(c) <u>Allocation to Class 'A' trades for training</u>

Full consideration will be given to any preference expressed on AF B 59 when deciding the trade in which the boy is to be trained. The decision, however, must be primarily determined by his aptitude and progress in comparison with other candidates and in relation to the number of vacancies in each trade.

(d) <u>Transfer to corps after training</u>

It must be clearly understood that whilst every endeavour will be made to appoint the candidate at the end of his training to one of the corps selected and entered by him on AF B 59, no guarantee can be given that this will be done, as such appointment will depend on his suitability and the requirements of the army at the time.

ENLISTMENT

10. (a) After the examination, boys will return to their homes and await the results, which will be notified to them as early as possible. Candidates for enlistment will be selected in order of merit from those who obtain a qualifying standard at the entrance examination. They will be provisionally allotted to trades according to the requirements of the army, their place in the examination and their own wishes.

    (b) Successful candidates will be enlisted into the Regular Army between 5th and 7th September, 1950'

    (c) Boys allotted vacancies as apprentice chefs will be enlisted direct into the Army Catering Corps. All other boys allotted vacancies will be enlisted into the General Service Corps.

TERMS OF SERVICE

11. (a) The terms of service will be to serve with the colours up to the age of 18 years and thereafter for a period of 8 years with the colours and 4 years with the Royal Army Reserve, or for 12 years with the colours. The boy may choose either of these alternatives when he is enlisted.

    (b) Attestation will be carried out on AF B 271. Before proceeding with the attestation the army recruiting officer will hand to the boy a copy of the Notice Paper (AF B 271A) which sets out the terms and conditions under which he will be enlisted and he will ensure that the boy understands them. (Parents may ask to see this form and check it for themselves at any time before the boy is enlisted).

PERIODS OF TRAINING

12. The period of training in Army Apprentice Schools is as follows:-

    <u>Class 'A' apprentice tradesmen</u> – 3 years, followed by a period of continuation training according to trade.

    <u>Class 'B' apprentice tradesmen</u> – 18 months, after which they will be available for transfer to corps for the balance of their training.

    <u>Apprentice chefs in Army Catering Corps</u> – Approximately 3 years.

TRADE EFFICIENCY

13. (a) A boy enlisted for training as an apprentice tradesman who, after reasonable trial, is considered unlikely to become an efficient tradesman in his trade, will be liable to be trained in another trade, relegated to non-tradesman class in a different unit, or discharged under instructions from the War Office.

A Sin to Tell a Lie
APPRENTICES CONDITIONS OF ENTRY, 1950

(b) No apprentice tradesman under the age of 18 years will be relegated to the non-tradesman class of trumpeter, bugler, or drummer without his agreement and that of his parents or guardian. After attaining the age of 18 years, however, a soldier enlisted as an apprentice tradesman fails to pass the qualifying test or who is considered unsuitable for further trade training, is liable to be retained in the service as a non-tradesman.

DISCHARGE BY PURCHASE

14. Discharge by purchase under para 390 (vii) of King's Regulations, 1940 "Having claimed discharge under section 81 Army Act" is open to boys enlisted for training as apprentice tradesmen, provided application for discharge is made and purchase money (£20) is paid within three months of the date of attestation. After these first three months a larger sum has to be paid, increasing with the length of service.

RATES OF PAY

15. The rates of pay are as follows :-

On enlistment	1s. 6d, per day
After 1 year	2s. 0d, per day
After 2 years	2s. 6d, per day
On attaining age 17½ years	4s. 0d, per day (mans normal recruit rate)

Subsequent pay will be at the current rate for men

ACEPTANCE OF CONDITIONS

16. The parents or legal guardian of a boy will be required to accept these conditions of entry by signing AFB 59 before the boy is enlisted into the Regular Army.

17. DO ASK YOUR LOCAL RECRUITNG OFFICER FOR HELP IF YOU NEED IT. They know what a big decision it is for parents or guardians to decide on a career for their son. They will do anything to help and are there to give information and explain any details that may seem difficult.

The War Office,
London, S.W.1.

27/Misc/7937/AG10

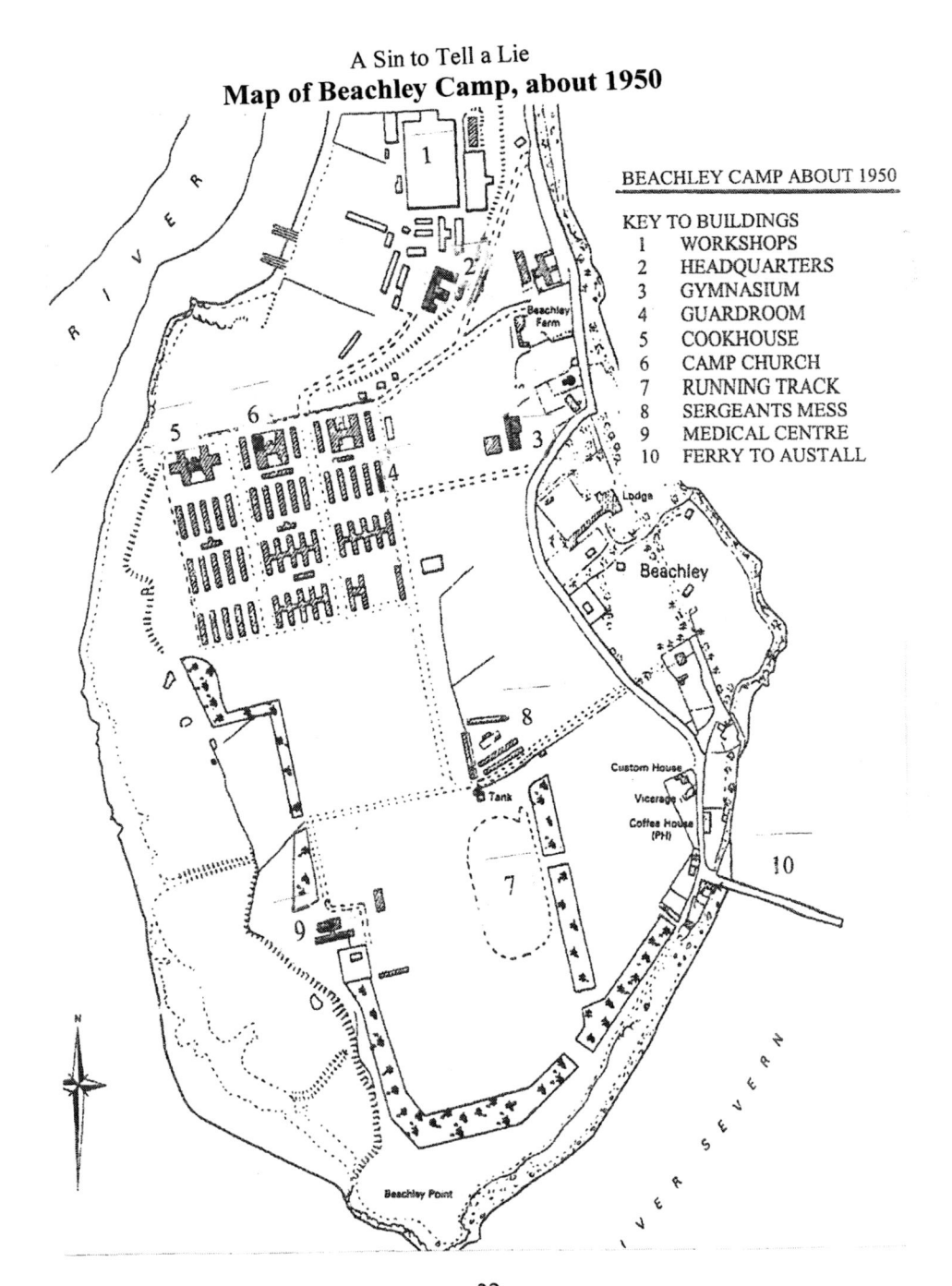

A Sin to Tell a Lie
Map of Beachley Camp, about 1950

BEACHLEY CAMP ABOUT 1950

KEY TO BUILDINGS
1. WORKSHOPS
2. HEADQUARTERS
3. GYMNASIUM
4. GUARDROOM
5. COOKHOUSE
6. CAMP CHURCH
7. RUNNING TRACK
8. SERGEANTS MESS
9. MEDICAL CENTRE
10. FERRY TO AUSTALL

A Sin to Tell a Lie
Attestation Form

COPY OF REGULAR *Certified true* ARMY ATTESTATION

Army No. DWEB 1.74
Corps. CSC
Nature of Engagement (see Note 1) NORMAL
EIGHT years with Colours FOUR years with Reserve
WEF Allowing 18 years of age.

QUESTIONS TO BE PUT TO THE RECRUIT BEFORE ENLISTMENT

1. What is your full name? (a) First names John Patrick (b) Surname DURKAN.
2. Where were you born? Parish — Town Croydon County Surrey.
3. What is your nationality? Brit/Eng
4. What was the nationality at birth of:— (a) Yourself? Brit/Eng (b) Your father? Brit/Eng (c) Your mother? Brit/Eng (d) Your wife? —
5. What is your trade or calling? School boy
6. (a) What was your age in years last birthday? 15 (b) State 20 day 4 month 1935 year of birth
7. (a) Are you single, married, widowed, divorced? (State which) Single
   (b) How many children are dependent on you? None
8. DO YOU NOW BELONG TO, OR HAVE YOU EVER SERVED in the Naval, Military or Air Forces of the Crown or in any Dominion or Colonial Force? (See note 2.) No.
9. Have you truly stated the whole, if any, of your previous service? Yes
13. (a) Into what corps do you wish to enlist? CSC

Army Form B 271B

REGULAR ARMY ATTESTATION — ADDITIONAL LIABILITIES
(These conditions do NOT apply to recruits enlisting for colour service only)

1. What is your full name? (a) First names (b) Surname.
   (a) JOHN PATRICK (b) DURKAN.
2. ARE YOU WILLING TO SERVE ON THE FOLLOWING CONDITIONS... Yes
3. Have you received a copy of this form? Yes

Date 6th Sept 1950 Signature of Recruit John Patrick Durkan Signature Witness Robinson

Yes

BRIGHTON.

This lad claims to be unattached, with no convictions or responsibilities, solvent and truthful! Let's be honest about this - would anyone in their right mind with so many virtues want to join up in the first place?!? So what had he been up to?

A Sin to Tell a Lie

Beachley Humour

When RSM 'Busty' Baker retired in 1954, having been the staff RSM for seven years, he was in the time honoured way dined out by the Warrant Officers & Sergeants Mess, Beachley Camp. In his farewell speech he related the following.

"....This afternoon the Colonel did me the honour of saying that a great deal had been achieved over the last seven years – and I must take my share of blame for it! He asked me what I felt epitomised that progress. Will someone kindly explain what that word means to Staff Jenkins – it has got damn all to do with buggery! As I was saying, the Colonel asked my view. This is what I said.

Sir, when I arrived here the lavatories had a supply of old newspapers, six months later we had the papers pre-cut into eight inch squares. Then restrictions were lifted and we threaded the paper on string and hung it on nails. When things improved we were issued with square toilet paper. Things got better when a grateful nation decided we could have the luxury of toilet rolls and some time later they gave us roller frames which we fitted to the doors with the redundant nails. I cannot recall what happened to the string but no doubt it was retrieved by some dim clerk from the QM stores, recorded and returned to the depot for recycling! But that was not the end of progress because the toilet rolls got bigger and softer and now, as I reach the end of my service career, I get nothing but complaints because the rolls are too bloody big for the holders! So you see, Sir, we have made considerable progress and our toilets are fit for an officer's bottom, at last.

Thank you all and good luck for the future."

The RQMS stood, "On behalf of us all I wish to thank RSM Baker for his kind words, in particular those words about the QM stores. As one Coldstream Guardsman to a brother

Grenadier, he may rest assured that wherever he goes and whatever he does in his new career in Civvy Street, I shall always think of him whenever I visit a shithouse...."

■■

The language of apprentices when together, especially in the sudden freedom of the early years, often left something to be desired. This swearing was endorsed to a degree, as in most macho societies, by the fact that soldiers are soldiers and the benevolence of military staff who had become accustomed to it in the stresses and strain of military action; but it was rarely used by the staff in a prolonged or an offensive way – drill sergeants may be cruel but foul language on parade was neither tolerated nor condoned. After all, the looks alone and the mocking sardonic comments concerning failure or inefficiency were enough to petrify us!

Apprentice Mole threw open the barrack room door, switched on the lights and swaggered in despite the fact that 'lights out' had been sounded. His voice rolled out.
"Fuck me, lads, I had a marvellous fuckin' time tonight! I took the Provo Sergeant's daughter to the fuckin' pictures, bought her an ice cream and lifted her fuckin' bra-zeer. Afterwards we fuckin' snogged in the Castle grounds and she put her fuckin' tongue right down my fuckin' throat. I took off her fuckin' knickers and laid her on the ground. Fuck me! I was in seventh fuckin' heaven. She couldn't keep her fuckin' hands off me."
A tired voice spoke up, "And what the fuck did you do then, Digger?"
"...Well..... I gave 'er one, didden I?"

A Sin to Tell a Lie
EARLY DAYS - POST CARDS HOME

"DO YOU KNOW WHAT BECOMES OF LITTLE BOYS WHO SWEAR?"
"YUS! THEY JOINS THE ARMY AND BECOMES SERGEANT-MAJORS!"

Dear Mum and Dad. Got here safely. Dad was wrong the Sergeant Major is human I think. The other boys are ok except one has stinky feet and another cries all night. I'm starving, please send food. We jus got a pay-rise but we can't have it in case we go absent without leave. Our SARGE is ok, he isn't our friend he tells us but he smiles at us when he calls us wankers. Love Johnny. PS Are piles catching?

A Sin to Tell a Lie
EARLY DAYS - POST CARDS HOME

'You will take your physical jerks under me tonight, Miss Ticklewell!'

Dear Mum & Dad, we have to make our own bed, crease our trousers an shave an polish our boots every day. I burned my boots now they leak. Theres a big scorch mark on my trousers. I know you think I'm just trying to get out but the room corporal keeps trying to kiss me goodnight because he wants to be a Sergint major. Why have you gone to live in Australia? Please send me 20 nicker so I can buy myself out. This place is like a prison camp. If you don't send the money I shall drink a bottle of Brasso. Jimmy

A Sin to Tell a Lie
EARLY DAYS - POST CARDS HOME

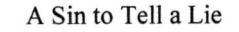

"YOU ARE SUPPOSED TO SALUTE WITH YOUR HAND!"

Dear Granny, you would be proud of me. We wear the same uniform as Grandad did in the trenches an' have the same rifle except we ave no bullets. The staff are all old fogies, lots are as old as you. I know Grandad got a shilling a day to be shot at - well we only get two shillings each week to be shouted at. The Sargint Major can swear but not as good as Grandad. Our heads have been scalped so we are not allowed out in case anyone sees us. Frankie

A Sin to Tell a Lie
EARLY DAYS - POST CARDS HOME

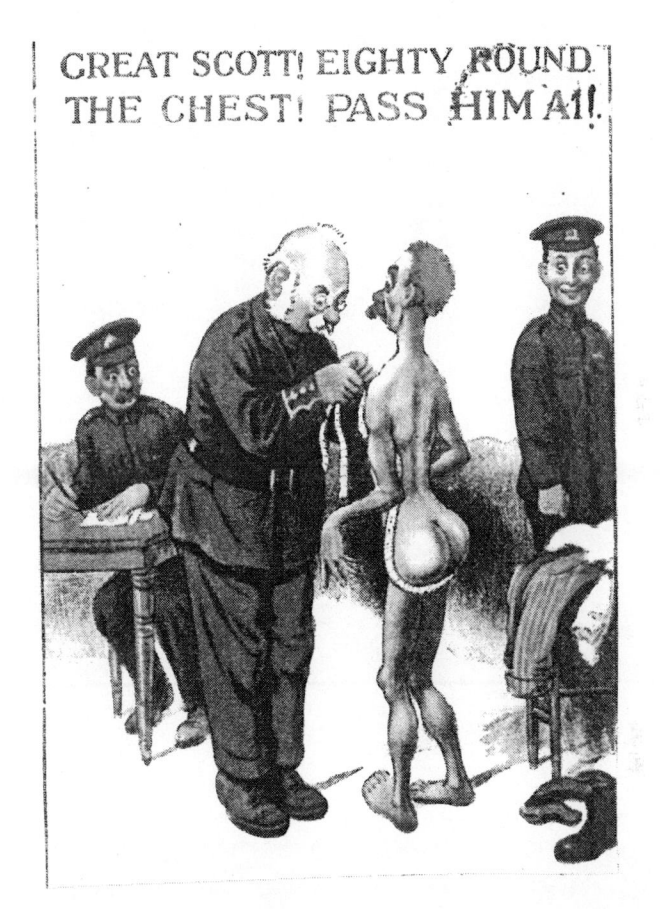

> GREAT SCOTT! EIGHTY ROUND THE CHEST! PASS HIM A1!

Dear mum,
      our Sarge swore at me when I ackci-dently stuck my bayonet in him. He asked me if I knew my father. When I sed no, he sed 'I bleedin well thought so.' I complained but he sed being fatherless would guarantee a successful army career and promotion. Your proud son - Arthur

A Sin to Tell a Lie
EARLY DAYS - POST CARDS HOME

BEACHLEY FERRIES ➡ THIS WAY

Dear Mum an Dad, My last letter was sent back Address Unknown. I know Borstal didn't cure me but Beachley has made a new lad of me. I promise ill be better. The Provo Sarge gave me this card of all the staff leaving camp when they heard I wasn't being discharged after I set fire to the guardroom. But after seven days on bread an water ill never do it again. Your lovin son - George. Ps Only kiddin about the staff.

A Sin to Tell a Lie
BEACHLEY PIN-UPS, 1950

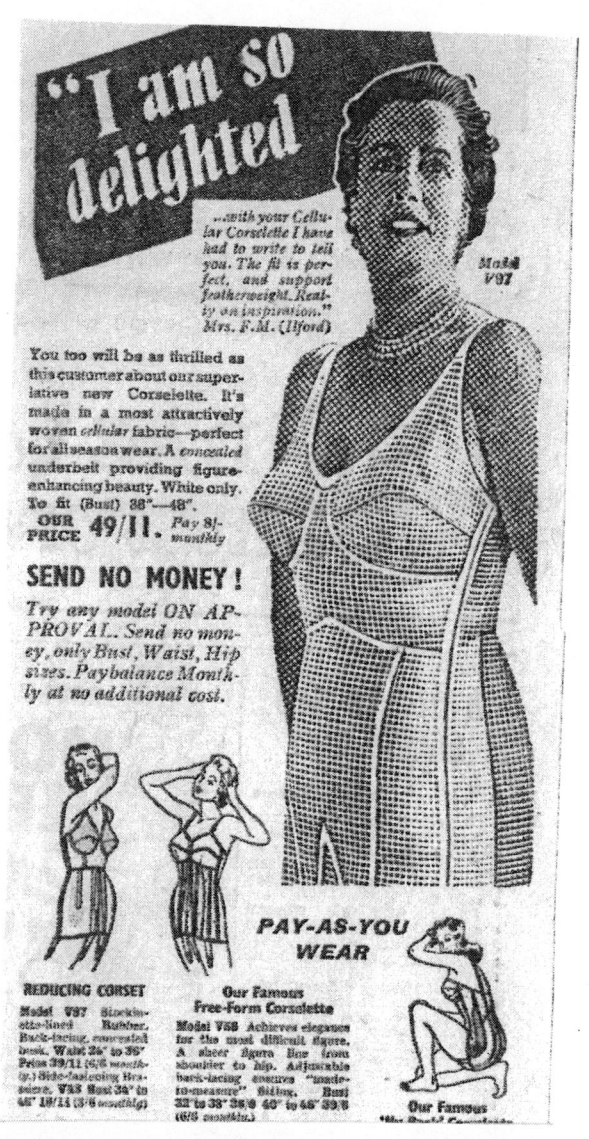

(Sorry lads, but there were no page 3 girls in 1950, this is page 1 of the adverts.)

A Sin to Tell a Lie
SPORTING PROWESS

Dear Mum & Dad, this is Joe winning the middle weight title. He also got 10 days jankers cos the Commandant said he'd let the school down as well as his shorts. We don't think he did though because he got a terrific cheer.   Your son Bill.   PS our C.O. fainted but his wife was OK. The NAAFI girls cheered and are giving Joe a buckshee tea!!!

A Sin to Tell a Lie
THE APPRENTICE'S LOT

LIFE IS FULL OF FUN AND LAUGHTER FOR THE ARMY APPRENTICE. COME TO BEACHLEY FOR A GREAT HOLIDAY AND BRACING HEALTHY WEATHER.

Dear Mum an Dad, my brain has overflowed three times already! - and there's still eighteen months left. I've told them that Dad was certified insane when he signed for me but they still wont let me go. Please send me a book on obscure diseases, Your son, Albert

A Sin to Tell a Lie
BOYHOOD HERO

BRYLCREEM your hair

Keeps hair in top form

For handsome, tidy hair that keeps its good looks all through the day, use Brylcreem, the perfect hair dressing. You can rely on Brylcreem to keep you right on top. For Brylcreem not only gives the hair life and lustre; the pure emulsified oils it contains tone up the scalp and prevent Dry hair and Dandruff. Brylcreem your hair and make smartness your goal. Brylcreem is in jars and tubes 1/11½d.

In 1950 one of our great boyhood heroes was Denis Compton, England cricketer and Arsenal footballer; in 1950 he won a FA Cup Winners medal with Arsenal. In a career seriously curtailed by the war he was a prolific batsman playing in 78 Test Matches. He was also an all-rounder taking 25 wickets and 49 catches for England.

Small wonder that every young lad wanted to 'Brylcreem' his hair!

A Sin to Tell a Lie
A BEACHLEY CHRISTMAS CARD

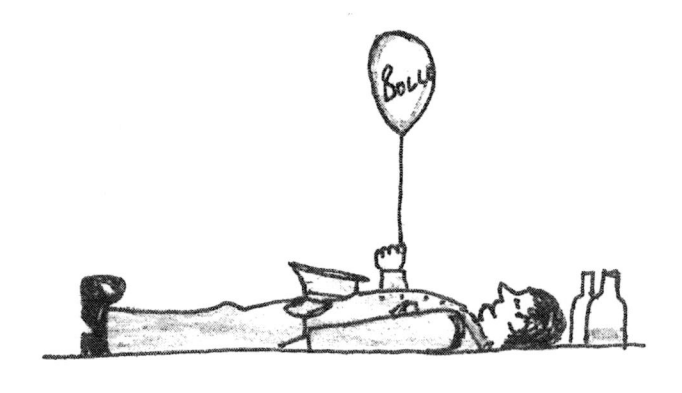

A MERRY CHRISTMAS FROM BEACHLEY

A Sin to Tell a Lie

SHUT THAT BLOODY DOOR!

A Sin to Tell a Lie
CHRISTMAS MENU 1951

ARMY APPRENTICES SCHOOL, BEACHLEY.

Christmas, 1951.

Menu.

Tea and Biscuits in Bed.

BREAKFAST.
Cornflakes and Hot Milk.
Fried Egg, Grilled Bacon, Grilled Sausage.
Grilled Tomato, Bread, Butter and Marmalade.
Tea or Coffee.

DINNER.
Cream of Tomato Soup.
Roast Turkey, Stuffing, Bread Sauce.
Braised Ham, Piquante Sauce.
Roast Beef and Gravy.
Brussels Sprouts, Green Peas.
Roast and Creamed Potatoes.

Christmas Pudding and Brandy Sauce.
Fruit and Nuts.
Lemonade.

HIGH TEA.
Cold Ham, Cold Roast Beef, assorted Meats and Salad.
Sausage Rolls, Bread and Butter.
Fruit Trifle, Jellies, etc.
Christmas Cake, Mince Pies.
Tea.

The Commandant and Staff wish you a Merry Christmas and a Prosperous New Year.

A Sin to Tell a Lie
A RECRUIT'S BEST FRIENDS!!!

"'OO SAID BULL IS BULLSHIT!"

A Sin to Tell a Lie

THE BRITISH ARMY

You may view the British Army in many ways. You may admire the splendour, the gallant history, the constant heroism or its steadfastness and professionalism; to highlight but a few of its virtues. We could go on.

But if you have been a soldier you may take a different perspective. You may rather think of comradeship, shared hardships and pleasures, the humour and the banter. You would also, most likely, recall the foolish stupidities, the crass orders and occasionally the pig-headed authority. If there is one thing you learn as a soldier, it is this – men rarely become infallible or even good leaders overnight. Often they struggle to cope with unaccustomed authority, incapable of moderating or reversing bad decisions even when the need is obvious and clear! At other times they stick to the old way, the 'tried and true' and ignore the need for essential change.

Out of all these myriad events and daily trials the British Soldier learns how to cope no matter what and with his courage undiminished; maintaining unshakeable good spirits that overcome all adversities and the idiosyncrasies of 'orders'. But soldiers rarely forget, even if they forgive – and in those memories we find the old soldier's stories. But they also rarely condemn for those were their days – their times. Far off days that can never be repeated but relived in the telling of their yesterdays.

A Sin to Tell a Lie

PASSING OUT

PARADE

THE SCHOOL BRASS BAND

A Sin to Tell a Lie

Captain Marsden's Carafe

February, 1950

'Sorry, old chap, but there it is. Now the war is over we're not wanted any more, really - neither you nor I – that's the truth of it. See you started in 33, in the jolly old depression. Plenty of wartime action; God, how 'Gerry' plastered us as we tried to push the tanks through to the bridge at Arnhem. Good old Monty, eh! Those were the days; you led the regiment for three months after that because poor old Colonel Billy Coe copped it. Those were the days, indeed. I know you want to stay on for your pension but its back to Lieutenant I'm afraid – yes, I know that's back to 39, Ronnie, but.... What's the alternative? You can take your demob and finish now with a few quid in

A Sin to Tell a Lie

your pocket or stay on and serve here; but there will be no promotion in the foreseeable future - junior officers are two a penny. Oh! - Sorry you feel like that! Any other options? Well, there is one but I doubt very much you'll like it; I feel a bit of a cad even mentioning it. Position in an army school for boys, you see. Rank of Captain naturally but it's a dead end – complete full stop old chap, no way out or back. Keep your nose clean and you'll get your pension but nothing else. What's the job? Oh, company commander of a company of boys. You'll take it! My God, do you know where it is! It's in the arse-end of...'

Ronnie Marsden, actually Captain Ranald Keith Marsden in honour of some romantic ancestry that existed only in his mother's mind that is, of the Royal Tank Regiment, and now Company Commander of C Company, slipped out of his reverie as a cyclist sped by. The view from his office window was a black wall surmounted by a black roof under a leaden grey sky. There was a narrow road between his window and the wall, but he couldn't see that from his chair. The cyclist had obviously been keen to get out of the rain that was just starting; he was most likely the H.Q. orderly room runner with today's letters and Part 1 and 2 Orders. No doubt the CSM and the company clerk would scrutinise them for every scrap of useless information, they had as little to do as he had, before passing them to him. He picked up a glass and filled it from his carafe. It was a modest cut glass carafe but nonetheless he was quite proud of it. A poor imitation of the Tank Corp badge was etched on the body. The carafe had been presented to him at a mess dinner on his last evening with the regiment, so while he realised that it had no great intrinsic value he held it in high esteem. Nearly as high as the esteem with which he was regarded by the regiment he had been told; but at least he held to his esteem whereas they had forgotten him by the next morning. That probably explained why he never received an

A Sin to Tell a Lie

'OUR FARVER, I JOINED THE ARMY TO SEE THE WORLD BUT ALL I'VE SEEN IS BEACHLEY. IT'S NOT FAIR. I WISH I'D JOINED THE BOY SCOUTS AT LEAST THEY GO TO CAMP AND HAVE JOLLY SONGS – AN THEY DON'T HAVE A SARNT MAJOR WHO KEEPS THROWING FITS...'

A Sin to Tell a Lie

invitation to Bovingdon and his old mess dinners. As he sipped his water he thought about today's end of afternoon meeting with the Commandant, Colonel Peter. On most Friday afternoons the company commanders assembled in the Colonel's office to make short positive reports. The Colonel's office was in the Admin Block, the only decent modern building in the camp, and that had been built by the apprentices! Colonel Peter liked positive reports that veered towards the evangelical. Ronnie had one hundred and sixty five boys in his company and he could say without fear of contradiction that he disliked almost every one of them. Not so Colonel Peter who seemed to have an abiding affection for the whole blooming lot, even the ones with two left legs, who grew out of their uniform overnight and had a tendency to ignore or blow kiss-waves at King's Regulations. New batches of boys were to be distributed from Headquarters Company in a few days time. HQ Company was where the boys were placed for the first six months of their service. Ostensibly this was to ensure they were properly evaluated, inducted and given basic training in an appropriate environment. In reality it was to prevent the slaughter of the innocents by their peers, i.e. larger boys with greater appetites, superior strength and a tendency to look down on anyone with less service than they had. The baiting of 'rookies' was forbidden but the little fellahs were safer if they were kept partly isolated for the first six months. Another bunch of neer do wells, brimming with the bloody optimism of youth and no fucking responsibilities, thought Ronnie. Still, with each new bunch his pension day grew ever closer. If only the cookhouse really would put bromide in the mashed potato as well as the tea! They would eat anything and everything. Every other camp had a pig swill man whose payments boosted the mess funds. Not here. The boys passed through the cookhouse like a plague of locusts. Put these thoughts from your mind, Ronnie, he thought. The apprentices who had just left were a decent bunch of triers. The Company had more than its fair share of Polish émigré lads who excelled at sports if not in the classroom. But that did not matter because attainment in education did not count for 'Champion Company' and with only modest luck this prize was within his grasp this coming summer. That was worth a few plaudits from the old Colonel, by jove. It certainly took the critical edge from the annual review with the Colonel. After all was said and done, Champion Company was about soldiering and discipline, not all this technical piffle and tradesmen waffle.

There was a sharp tap on the door and Company Sergeant Major Harry Kidd of the Somerset Light Infantry, stepped in. In his hand he held the recently delivered post, so he had an official reason for entry. Naturally that was not the real reason for his entry. In reality he wanted to ensure that dear Ronnie was sober enough to attend the Commandant's meeting.

"The official correspondence, Sir. The RSM called to say the Commandant is running late, Sir." As he spoke he searched his officer for signs of inebriation, apart that is from the obvious red veins that ran across his nose and upper face like class A roads on an Ordnance Survey Map. Despite the fact that one of the CSM's eyes was blackened and half closed and the opposite cheek was bruised, there was no condemnation in this examination; after all was said and done, this was his C.O.; a man who deserved and got his loyalty, right or wrong. CSM Kidd did not mind being incarcerated here at Beachley. In fact he wouldn't have minded getting drunk now and again either but caught between piss-poor pay and a careful Mrs Kidd, that was impossible. The CSM's eye had been blackened in the line of duty. Yesterday evening the Captain had decided to gee-up the company boxing team with a bit of inspirational and direct coaching. After all it was important to win every trophy if they were to be 'Champion Company'. Ronnie had done a bit of boxing in his day. Unfortunately for the CSM, Ronnie needed a partner to demonstrate the pugilistic art of offence and self defence. Naturally the last thing the CSM wanted to do was prance around a bloody boxing ring being thumped by an over enthusiastic boxer demonstrating his left hook especially when he was constrained by the thought that he may be liable to be court-martialled if he clouted the sod in return. Luckily for him the boys were quick learners so he only got thumped twice before being allowed to retire. His wife had not helped either as she had threatened to blacken the other eye if he was stupid enough to enter a boxing ring again at his age.

"Thank you, Sar'nt Major," Captain Marsden glanced out of the window, "seems like I was wise to bring my raincoat. If my wife calls, tell her I'll be late."

"Right, Sir. Company kit inspection in the morning, Sir. And there are two lads on charges."

"Apprentices, Sar'nt Major, apprentices," he shook his head slowly a few times to underline the censure. "Nothing interesting or salacious I hope, like rape, beastiality or sodomy." He tried not to sound overly hopeful.

"Goodness gracious me, Sir," The CSM was deeply shocked. "Nothing like that, Sir."

Bollocks, thought Ronnie, that would have given old Gammy Peter something to worry about. He helped himself to a drop of water from his carafe. The CSM peered at the carafe with X-Ray eyes as if he was convinced it held something stronger than water. No, CSM Kidd, Ronnie thought, there is no gin in my carafe and more's the pity. He recalled the last meeting he had had with the Colonel. *'I trust you are happy here at Beachley, Ronnie?' 'Yes, sir, absolutely fuckin' ecstatic! Most fulfilling, Sir.'* It was not only best to lie but his pension depended on it. *The Colonel pontificated as Colonels were wont to do, 'We must do our best for these lads, you know; in a few years they will be running the army. Our legacy.' 'Of course,' he had replied, 'we must shape and guide them like*

A Sin to Tell a Lie

"NO YOU CAN'T HAVE 'MEN ONLY' FOR THE PADRE! HE HASN'T RETURNED THE LAST TWO COPIES."

true professionals' 'Well said, I couldn't have put it better myself, I must remember those words'

Ronnie had shut his eyes and prayed that Germany would rearm before it was too late. Perhaps another war would save him but his hope had withered when the Colonel had undertaken his last appraisal with a daunting forecast. Our days of active service are over, Ronnie, we are only the tenuous guardians of the future – others must fight the battles, if there are any, which I doubt somehow. Even he had looked disappointed as he said it. Ronnie remembered what the Padre had said - *we are custodians of these boy's bodies and souls because they are full of potential sin. Without restraint they would outshine and certainly out-sin the devil.* Yes, guide and shape, he thought, guide and shape the little sods and keep them from sinful sin, even if they prayed for it every night on bended knees in total sincerity, which he was convinced they did.

The telephone sounded in the outer office and the clerk, Sergeant Swift, called out, "That was the RSM. Colonel's meeting in five minutes, Sir." Ronnie wondered why the RSM used the phone. Even when soliciting marital favours from his wife he could be heard quite distinctly at a hundred paces. Were Grenadier Guardsmen partially deaf like old tankmen? Thank goodness the old buffer hadn't joined the tanks he reflected; they would never have got him inside one. RSM Baker was 78 inches – up and round!

"I'm on my way. Sar'nt Major, make sure my carafe is cleaned and refilled with fresh water." He stomped out into the rain. Another week nearly over. Then he remembered there was a kit inspection in the morning. Oh fucking joy, rows of pristine useless bits of equipment the lads kept for show only, while the things they actually used were carefully hidden. Did they really think he was fooled? There was no point in asking, they were even more accomplished liars than he was. As he made his way

A Sin to Tell a Lie

down the hill he glared heavenwards for a moment. Bastard! The rain increased as if to teach him manners. Halfway down the hill he met the only sign of life so far, a small squad of apprentices marching up, draped in waterproof groundsheets. The Apprentice NCO ordered the eyes right and saluted smartly; the drill was impeccable. He raised his right hand in reply. The thought crossed his mind that maybe a good job was being done. He doubted the Guards could have carried it off better. Yes, he lifted his head, pride was so important. Perhaps they were doing a good job with these lads. As the thought crossed his mind the rain stopped and a weak sun emerged, a sure sign that the almighty approved but not enough to start a major war! Dammit!

Back in the office Sergeant Swift, known to all as 'Speedy', typed out Company Orders detailing tomorrow's parades and official activities. As he did so he thought about the Saturday night dance in the Gymnasium. The outgoing group 48A was leaving in a few days and the dance on Saturday was their farewell; as usual the 'Sergeant Swift Quintet' had been chosen to orchestrate events. He looked forward to that. At seventeen pounds an evening that was a nice little earner for him and his fellow bandsmen; his lion's share of five pounds tax free exceeded his weekly pay and it was rare for a week to pass by without getting two bookings. Thank God there was fuck all else to do on a Saturday evening in Wales was his considered view! It was a pity that dances weren't allowed on Sundays because there was absolutely buggerall to do on a Sunday. The Welsh were a miserable lot was his considered opinion. Once you crossed the bridge into Chepstow on a Sunday every pub was shut! In his view they could, and should, have fornicated and danced the day away but no, all pleasures were forbidden. He thanked gawd for his dear old Mum who had believed in pleasure and insisted he learn the piano. The School had its

A Sin to Tell a Lie

own brass and drum bands but they couldn't play decent dance music to save their lives. As his fingers skipped along the keyboard Speedy found himself quietly humming. This was the life, a nice cushy job and plenty of money. May it go on for ever until his pension was due.

Tap tap tap – tap tap tap - *'Please be true - when you say -I love you – it's a sin to tell a lie……….'*

Safely tucked away in his little wooden hut just up the road, opposite the NAAFI, Bing the Barber stood gazing out of the window. He noted that the sun had emerged. On a more normal day he would have expected customers, every boy had to attend for a short back and sides once every fortnight or risk deportation, flogging, imprisonment or, even worse – a 'Bing Special'. But today they would avoid him like the plague, even risk retribution, as long as they could go to the end of term dance with flowing 'Brylcreemed' locks.

Bing was an efficient barber and could shave a head in under a minute but as a hair stylist he lacked flair, skill and hirsute creativity. He was not known as the 'demon barber' by the boys for nothing. Not only did he destroy the lads' hair but they paid for the privilege by a deduction from pay! Once in a while, without rancour or conscience, he recalled the day he had been appointed. Naturally he had lied. His training consisted of two hours hirsute butchery in Cardiff Prison before he was shown the exit gate but Beachley was not so fussy. Also his wife could help him and was only exposed to potential rather than convicted felons. She was a kindly soul really but being even uglier than her husband she had a tendency to avoid exposing her lack of social graces and feminine appeal by firmly keeping her mouth shut. Bing examined his list. "Put the kettle on, my love." She silently disappeared without a word, like a magician's assistant. Twenty lads hadn't signed in. That would be ten shillings off his wages if left uncorrected, so he carefully ticked each one and made a squiggle. If the little sods got caught out, well that was their hard luck. Later, when the RSM passed by on his way home Bing could report all correct and accounted for, Sergeant Major. He blessed the day he had got this job. Customer satisfaction! Bollocks! 780 haircuts guaranteed every fortnight at sixpence each, a few haircuts for staff that still had hair and no self respect, with free lodgings thrown in and no overheads. Plus the profit from the prophylactics. Just work that out. No wonder the RSM got a free one! Are you happy here, Mr Crosby? Not 'alf, Sir. And that's no bleedin' lie. He switched on his radio, humming happily to himself as he considered a cruise on the Queen Mary. Surely the wife could cope on her own for a fortnight while he took a well deserved break.

The C Company CQMS, Staff Sergeant Hector McCloud, stepped out of the store and double locked the door. It had been a hard day even though there was only one customer and a minor inventory check to intrude on his leisure. There was only one certainty he was aware of – the Army was never going to make him rich, so he must seek consolation and wealth elsewhere. He had whiled away much of the time praying for the 'Midas Heavenly Touch' to shower him with wealth and in between times he fervently checked the weekend's racing detail in the 'Racing Times'. He was a great believer in form; also the Sporting Gazette, the juxtaposition of Mars relative to Chepstow Castle, Captain Hargreaves of the Standard, his winkle pin, the number of outsize bloomers Mrs McCloud hung out to dry, the number of broken lampshades that could be charged and reclaimed as 'barrack-room damages' and sheer unadulterated luck. It was well known in the inner circles of betting that all of these methods worked; the difficult part was in knowing which one to follow on the day. He had also spent some considerable time perusing the Daily Mirror racing page and listening to the radio. As a well known betting aficionado, with a suitably discreet manner, he had several illegal bets from other hopefuls in his pocket ready for the local bookie. One of these days he would hit the jackpot; of that he was convinced, all he needed was a seven winner accumulator at an average of seven to one and could retire to the Bahamas. He sauntered down to the company office and looked in.

"You ready Speedy?" The bus would leave for the married quarters in fifteen minutes.

"Just a mo. Got a winner for tomorrow?"

"Always got a winner, Speedy. That's why they call me 'Lucky Q'."

Now there's a fucking lie, thought Speedy, you'd be better off sticking to bingo.

CSM Kidd put his beret on, "Wait for me. Must speak to the Orderly Corporal first."

He disappeared into the back office.

"I see he's got his Jack and Jill books ready for the weekend," the CQMS observed. CSM Kidd was due to sit his Army Second Class Certificate of Education on Monday so he was going to swot all over the weekend. During the war he had found no difficulty in learning weapons and bayonet drill and imparting that knowledge to others but it had come as a shock when the Army decided that a modest educational standard was mandatory for peacetime promotion. Does 4 come after 3? The drill sergeant's mantra, one – two, three – one, had sufficed for years.

Speedy sounded mournful, "I hope he passes this time. The lads can't stop chuckling when he fails. How can a man who can break down, repair and reassemble a bleedin' Bren Gun in the dark with his bollocks nearly blown off, about to be bayoneted by mad Japs and under heavy shellfire, fail a simple arithmetic test?"

The CQMS smiled, "Is that how he got his Military Medal?"

"No, he shot several smartarse storemen."

"I may only be a storeman but I've got more sense than to go boxing with a bloody maniac. Before the war he was called 'Ragin' Ranald' by the Tankies you know."

Speedy grimaced. "He'll get over it, and there are no broken bones. You coming to the dance tomorrow?"

"Not likely. I don't want my wife and daughter being molested by a bunch of oversexed lads."

"Your daughter may enjoy it," he said; but your old missus is safe I reckon, he thought.

In the rear office CSM Kidd glared at the Orderly Corporal. "I want to see my face in that lino in the morning – and if the C.O's carafe doesn't gleam I shall push my pace stick up your nose and poke about until you can whistle 'Dixie' through it."

Still February, 1950

Joseph Kinson was extremely lucky. At his medical the orderly had measured his height. "Just under, Sir. Four six and

A Sin to Tell a Lie

seven eighths." And he's stretching himself, he thought. Four feet seven was the official entry height. The Medical Officer had looked up from his notes. "Uum-m. He seems well enough. Make it four seven, he'll grow a bit before he gets to the school." Then he looked intently at Joseph. "I want you to hang from the bars twice a day for ten minutes - is that clear? Good."

That had been over a week ago. The train pulled into Chepstow station. Joseph was quite relieved because he had had to sit on the edge of the seat for the whole journey so his toes could touch the floor. Luckily he was wearing his first pair of long trousers so that prevented his legs from being chafed. It had been a terrible long journey all the way from Essen in Germany. He turned to his companion, "We're there, Vic."

Vic reached up for the pitifully small cardboard suitcases and lowered them down while Joseph dropped the window and opened the door. They gingerly stepped down onto the platform. As they gazed about the empty platform the whistle blew and the train pulled away leaving them lonely and a trifle forlorn.

CHEPSTOW RAILWAY STATION- GATEWAY TO BEACHLEY.

"Where do we go from here?" Vic looked puzzled, "I'm hungry."

Thirty yards off a smartly dressed Sergeant, wearing a red sash, looked out of the waiting room door and seeing them called out with a wave, "This way you lads!"

Joseph and Vic never voiced the immediate question that crossed their minds. 'How does he know us?'

"What's your names?" His pencil hovered over his tally board.

Vic took charge, "I'm Church and he's Kinson."

The sergeant looked at Joseph suspiciously, "Are you sure you're for Beachley?"

"Yes, Sergeant. I enlisted two days ago."

The Sergeant turned away muttering; "Fuck me, I 'ope the army bleedin' well knows what it's doing! Follow me."

The bus in the yard was already half full. A very tall skinny lad looked at Joseph, "You can sit here if you like. What's your name?"

"Joseph – but my friends call me Joe."

"I'm Mike. Mike Kimber."

Joe looked up at him, "You're tall!"

"I was the tallest boy in my school. Were you the smallest?"

"Of course not! There were lots of boys in the first and second years smaller than me."

The receiving sergeant motioned the driver to depart, "I can't wait to get to camp. That lad back there is as tall as Busty Baker – and he's only fifteen! He'll be the only person in the camp who can look Busty straight in the eye."

"Yeah, but what about the little one, eh? He could shelter under Busty Baker's belly and never get wet!"

"We have a duty to his parents to ensure he is never put in such danger." The Sergeant started humming as he sat down.

A Sin to Tell a Lie

'Bless 'em all, bless 'em all, the long and the short and the tall,
Bless all the sergeants and double-u-o ones……..'

'WELCOME TO BEACHLEY, LAD.'

Joseph interrupted him, "How far is it, Sarge?"
"Sergeant to you lad, an' don't you forget it. About twenty minutes"
"Sorry Sergeant – my Dad's in the army."
"Your Dad's in the army and you still wanted to join?"
"I like working with my hands, Sergeant."
"Well, for your information I shall be your platoon sergeant and I want no hanky-panky - do you hear me! You will sleep with your hands outside your pyjamas and your bedclothes where they can be seen at all times. No wonder you're so bloody small!"

A Sin to Tell a Lie

Dear Mum & Dad,, I'm a real Soldier now. Despite dad's fears I have not been put in the Guard-Room for answering back and I eat all my dinner. The Sarn't Major said I may be short but he can see his face in my boots. Joe.

May 1950

Mr Wallis lit a cigarette; he found that it helped his concentration when dealing with a difficult lad. Unfortunately the combination of smoking and concentration caused him to frown. This was often useful to a policeman in provoking a confession from a guilty suspect. Unfortunately the lad sat opposite was his son. "Your mum's been gone near on five years….." he faltered to a halt.

Peter sat very still, "I know Dad……I can hardly remember her." He wondered what this meeting was about but in the back of his mind lurked the knowledge that his step-mother had become somewhat hostile since his coming back from boarding school – and the feeling was reciprocated.

Mr Wallis fingered his cigarette, "I wish things had been different son - you know - what with the war and your mum leaving us so soon," he found the words were so hard to say, "life has been a bit shitty…me being away so long and….and me getting married again to..." He felt a great desire to explain that; about a man's need for support and comfort but realised it would sound selfish. Since returning home from the boarding school at Easter it was obvious that Peter and his new mother would never get on, never in a month of Sundays. "Have you anything in mind for the future?"

Peter nodded, "Perhaps I could join the merchant navy, I could…."

"I don't think that would be wise – no proper training – drifting about."

"I'm fifteen, Dad."

"I know. I want you to take an examination to join the army. The apprentice schools take lads from fifteen – proper training. What do you think?"

"I dunno, Dad …..Might be alright I suppose."

"I've put your name forward. The exams are next week." There was an awkward silence until Mr Wallis spoke again, "You'll be OK. After years in a home for - for waifs and strays, it'll be a piece of cake!" He wondered if he should put his arm around his son but found that he couldn't do it – but after all was said and done he told himself, it was hardly right for two men to show affection like that, so very unmanly. No, much better to maintain a decent reserve and the moment passed. "That's agreed then."

June 1950

Number One Platoon, Headquarters Company, had been rousted out onto parade in record time. One poor lad had his flies still open and a wet stain on his trousers; such was the force and speed with which he had been propelled from the toilet block! Luckily it was a warm day so the extent of the 'undressed-ness' was unlikely to cause great harm. An incandescent CSM about to emulate the fireworks display for the 1812 Overture however was another matter. The poor man was red from rage and exertion as he harassed the boys into line. "Three ranks! – For gawds sake three fuckin' ranks! STANDSTILL!"
Blessed silence descended for a few moments as he fought to control his anger. It could not last. His eyes bulged, his voice soared and his blood pressure hit 180 over 100.
"WHO DID THIS?" A piece of paper waved in his left hand. The last time a piece of paper had caused this degree of annoyance in the British Army had been the American Declaration of Independence. Twenty eight pairs of terrified eyes tried to focus ineffectually on the offensive document as a second wave of fear enveloped the platoon. The paper waved again. "MUTINY! Fuckin' mutiny I tell you!"

A Sin to Tell a Lie

With the greatest effort he managed to control himself. "Two of you wrote this letter of complaint. It seems that our food, accommodation and heating leave much to be desired! Field-Marshal Montgomery wishes to say in reply that he will not 'ave bleedin' petitions sent out in this way. You are fuckin' soldiers and soldiers experience hardships. A letter of complaint signed by more than one person is MUTINY! PUNISHABLE by DEATH! You miserable little buggers. Complaints made in this way defy King's Regulations as you well know. Worse still they defy me!"

He paused to peer around the platoon's twenty eight white and chastened faces. "Fahey! One step forward – march! Apprentice Day! One step forward – march!" His anger resurrected itself, "Come here you two!" They scuttled forward.

The letter appeared on the end of Fahey's nose, "Is that your signature, Fahey?"

A strangulated voice replied from low down, "Yessir."

"Did you write this letter?"

"No sir. I'm not good with letters."

A head bent down, "Are you shittin' yourself, Fahey?"

"Nosir."

"You will, lad – you will." The letter switched to Day, "Did you write and sign this letter?"

"Yessir."

"I've been in this man's army for twenty one years – d'you hear me, twenty one fuckin' years – and just when my pension is due, what is my reward –THIS! And to heap insult on injury you can't even spell properly. The Company Commander is waiting on you two; with his cane." For a brief moment a smile lit up his face – but it was the smile of the tiger. "Left turn! At the double – forward!........."

A Sin to Tell a Lie

July 1950

Dad opened the letter with the same care as a bomb disposal expert defusing a one ton mine. He was not used to receiving official looking letters from anyone except the Inland Revenue. Dad was a coalminer and he had never been allowed to serve in the war, even in the Home Guard, because of a deaf ear. After years of class warfare fighting the colliery owners and management he somehow, but misguidedly, thought that the army was a safe and benevolent place; even if a war had broken out in Korea and we were getting a pasting. We had seen Hitler off so a few 'chinks' couldn't be much trouble.

"It seems you passed! Have a look." He sounded pleased as he passed it to me. He was right. I suddenly felt elated. All those advertisements in the boys' comics and papers saying that the services wanted 'young men' to join up for a whole wonderful and exciting series of interesting and stimulating jobs on the advanced edges of skill and technology had won me over. See the world as well! Surely anything was better than a life in a small village serving the local coal mine. I really wanted to join the Navy to train as an artificer but that meant waiting another year whereas the Army wanted my body now. Mum was not so sure.

"You're a bit young to go off on your own," she tried to give Dad a signal but he ignored her so she persevered, "soldiers can be very rough you know."

"Oh, I don't think we need worry about that, Daisy, the letter from the Colonel and the advert said it's just like a public school. You can't say fairer than that, can you?"

Mum sniffed, "I've heard some funny things about public schools – very odd things! Besides which you can't believe advertisements – that pair of boots you bought fell to pieces in no time!"

A Sin to Tell a Lie

A Sin to Tell a Lie

Dad turned serious, "You don't have to go, son. Don't forget you've got your School Cert next summer. There'll be other opportunities, you know."

My heart sank; hope deferred makes the heart grow weak. "I'd rather go now, Dad. I'm fifteen."

"Once you're in there's no way out," he weakened, "but maybe I should have gone elsewhere when I was your age. Don't forget you have to tell the Headmaster."

The thought of telling Mr Myers, headmaster of the Grammar School, cooled my ardour. "I'll go to the office in the morning, Dad." I passed him the much thumbed job magazine the army had sent me, "That's what I want to do - the one on page five."

"You've to go for your medical next week so make sure you tell the school or I'll be getting another letter."

In my naivety I really thought that the examination had been a serious barrier to entry; it didn't occur to me until many years later that academic standards were of less importance than good health and a willingness to serve. Beyond that the Army had unparalleled faith in its ability to hammer dross into gilt if not gold on the heated anvil of the Army's training schemes. There was further evidence of my naivety when the medical orderly handed me a flask and asked me to fill it! I had no idea what he meant.

A Sin to Tell a Lie

"GOT ANYTHING ESCAPIST, Q?"

When Alice walked through the Looking Glass I doubt she was more unprepared than I was for what waited on the other side! In her case it was the Queen of Hearts – in my case, well! – more like the Ace of Clubs. It took the Army many years to accept the concept of shell shock, I don't believe it ever quite understood the shattering impact that first 3 days in the Army had on young lads. It was an alien world but boyish pride held most of us. To give in would mean admitting we had made a mistake. But then, as I came to realise, there were quite a few lads who had left far worse behind and to whom decent food, care and a chance to find a better place in life, the things they found at Beachley, were an absolute god-send.

A Sin to Tell a Lie

> **IF YOU THINK YOU'RE BRIGHT**
>
> **READ THIS**
>
> How's this for a life when you're young? Join an Army Apprentices School and you get first-class technical training (can be electronics or any of 40 T.U.C.-recognised trades). In the picture, an apprentice is servicing a radar presentation unit. You can earn while you learn. Board, lodging and uniform are free, and you get two months' paid holiday every year. Later you earn good money as a key technician in the New Army. It's a real man's life with a bunch of chaps your own age and the finest chances for sport in the world. These sprint cyclists are Army Apprentices. You could be setting the pace with them.
>
> **IF YOU'RE 14½–16½ POST THIS TODAY**
>
> To the War Office (MP6) London, S.W.1
> Please send me details about the Army Apprentices School (with no obligation on my part)
> NAME.. AGE......
> ADDRESS...
> TOWN........................ COUNTY..................
> Applications for the next Entry Examination must be in by May 12th, 1959.

Dear Mrs Kray,

    After due consideration of your application on behalf of your sons, I regret I cannot arrange for their transfer from Borstal. Whilst it is true that the Army encourages young recruits we much prefer to train apprentices via an approved scheme. Prior experience in arson, extortion, assault and battery, explosives and the use of weapons such as sawn off shotguns does not commend itself. I cannot answer for the Judge who commented on the 'professionalism' of your sons; whilst you may consider this to be praiseworthy, we much prefer to recruit and train in these skills those bright and talented young lads who have not, as yet, been caught and convicted.
   Yours Sincerely, General T. Roberts, MBE, Army Recruiting.

A Sin to Tell a Lie

July 1950 – 'Cheers! Cheers! The boys are here!'

Captain Marsden took another cigarette from his silver case and tapped the end to compact it; that completed he carefully put the case away and flicked his lighter. Ah, there was nothing like a Players fag to tickle the throat and steady his nerves, apart that is, from a large gin and tonic. Perched upon his shooting stick he had an excellent view of the track as the last critical athletic races got ready. If C Company won the inter-company athletics then the twenty points awarded would see them as 'Champion Company'. Ronnie dearly wanted that honour because the war in Korea was not going well and he was certain that he could persuade the Colonel to lobby on his behalf for a return to his regiment, with the champions trophy to his credit. How he yearned for that day. C Company was already leading in the meeting, having edged out the competition in the field events thanks to stalwart performances by his Polish lads who dominated the discus, javelin and jumps. But it was too early to become complacent. B Company had some fine runners and may yet pull back the lead. Over eight hundred staff and apprentices crowded around the track area giving it an almost carnival feel. The fine cinder oval track with four lanes was the school's pride and joy; it was reputed to be the only one for several hundred miles!

The loudspeakers crackled into life, *"Will the team captains report to the Marshal's tent immediately. The next event is the 2-20 yards relay and will be followed by the 4-40 yards relay."*

The results of the 100 yard event were added to the 'Score Board' and C Company's lead was eroded. Mrs Marsden, dragged here against her will, thought the result disgraceful.

A Sin to Tell a Lie

"What was that little devil doing, Ronnie?", she demanded, "letting you down like that."

The 'little devil' was hopping about in agony because someone had 'spiked' his ankle and all he could think of for the moment was that he may be so crippled that he would be unable to go on summer leave. He vented his anger on the offending competitor. "What the fuck did you do that for!" The offender looked hurt. "You got in front of me." "Corse I did, I was fuckin' winning, you c**t!"

CSM Kidd finished his pep talk to the relay teams, "Now I want you to go out there lads and destroy'em." He focussed on Lance Corporal Konopka, the final runner in both races. "If you don't win you'll be orderly bleedin' corporal from now 'til soddin' Christmas!"

There was a concerted shout as the first relay started; the crowd really tried to encourage the runners. The runners were neck and neck over the first two sections but the B Company runner in the third section had the edge by two yards as he rifled in towards the runner of the last lap; his baton outstretched. In an effort to close the gap the C Company runner overstretched himself and Konopka, eager to go, misjudged the pace. A horrified gasp went up as the baton dropped and a disconsolate Konopka threw his hands up in frustration. Captain Marsden was concerned as the rival points went up but he managed to appear nonchalant as the C Company lads redeemed themselves in the 4-40 relay. Two races to go, just the half mile and the mile. C Company needed to beat the B Company runners to stay in front. The B Company half-miler, Tom Hinton, was the favourite in that race.

Sergeant Swift knelt and massaged the calf of the C Company second string. "We gotta win this one, lad – you understand?"

"Dunno Sarge. Hinton has never lost."
"I reckon he's due for a fall, myself. When you bunch up on the first bend he might trip – terrible bad luck of course."
"I might get disqualified, Sarge!"
"Naw. Just bad luck as you bunch up. They never have marshals on the first bend. Just make sure – Hinton never goes for an early break."
"Dunno, Sarge. Sounds risky to me."
"I reckon if Hinton falls down someone could get five bob."

'Will the competitors for the half mile please report to the Marshal – the groundsman is required at the jumping pit. Spectators are reminded that dogs must be kept under strict control at all times.'

Speedy stared at heaven, "Half a crown now and the rest later."
A hand went out, "D'you reckon the Colonel's dog has shat in the sand again."
"Always does – every damn meeting. It's not a dog, it's a bleedin' camel!"

Bang! The half milers surged forward with long loping easy strides. Captain Marsden pulled his wife back to clear his view; behind his back he crossed his fingers. Silently he urged the runners on, his left hand tightly gripping his knee. There was hardly a stride between the five front runners but at this stage it didn't matter. This race would be decided in the last two hundred yards. He went to light a cigarette as a great roar went up, "What's happened?"
"A runner has fallen!"
Oh, my God, his teeth grated and he could barely look. An agitated wife screamed at him. "Who is it?"

A Sin to Tell a Lie

He stared at the runners now some hundred yards clear of the fallen boy. His spirits rose, his fists bunched; the two C Company lads were in the lead. They swept past as the bell sounded and the C Company Apprentice Sergeant Major orchestrated a tremendous cheer, "Come on C Company! C – C – C – C Company!"

As the runners came to the final bend Captain Marsden got to his feet for the first time this afternoon; he wanted to shout but no, that was bad form. But he could not suppress the feeling of ecstatic joy as the two C Company lads strode home first and second. Maximum points. B Company could never catch them now. He raised his hand in salute to Major Nash, the C.O. of B Company and mouthed 'hard luck'. Secretly he noted, with considerable pleasure and a straight face, that Major Nash looked thoroughly pissed off. Joy filled his heart. The Colonel was bound to speak so that would be his chance. His transfer request would be ready in the morning. Goodbye fuckin' Beachley.

The Apprentice CSM raised the silver cup as one hundred and sixty excited boys surrounded him. He knew, as they knew, that the sweet taste of success and victory was theirs to savour. They were the champion company, for the next term they would wear the crimson lanyard with pride. "Fall in C Company." The singing started.

"Cheers! Cheers! The boys are here,
what the hell do we care? – what the hell do we care?
Cheers! Cheers! The blacks are here.
Why the hell do we care now?
For we're a grand old lot to fight for,
For it's a grand old song we sing.
When you hear our history
It's enough to make your heart grow glad!, glad!, glad!
We don't care what the losers say,

A Sin to Tell a Lie

As on our way we go.
For we only know –that there's goner be a show
And the Black! - supporters will be there
They're at the NAAFI- queuing for the buckshee tea!

August 1950

The Magistrate adjusted his glasses and frowned. "Am I to understand that the accused has changed his plea?"

The solicitor tried to smile, it somehow made the plea seem more humanitarian, "Yes, sir. There are special circumstances that your Honour is unaware of and I wish to enter a mitigating plea."

"So he wishes to plead guilty, is that so? The charges are serious. This court cannot take the charges of assault and affray lightly."

"Yes, your Honour. But I ask that you hear the character witness and apology before deciding in this case. This young man left school at fifteen and since then has been unable to find proper employment and he has fallen in with bad company."

An army sergeant resplendent in immaculate uniform, his red sash in place, entered the witness box, removed his beret and took the oath.

"Please give your rank and name."

The heels clicked. "Recruiting Sergeant Parkes, London Recruitment Office, Sir."

"Will you please explain why you wish to speak on behalf of Church?"

"A month ago Church came to me and asked to enlist. That was not possible because of his age. However he later sat the Apprentices examination and passed. It was obvious from our discussion that he had been and still was in serious trouble but I believe he was entirely honest with me. The army is prepared to enlist him provided that he does not have a criminal record. Hence my plea that he be discharged and be allowed to serve his country."

"Are you not concerned at the gravity of the charges against him?"

"Channelled in the right direction, such characteristics are welcome in the army, sir. It is my firm belief that he is at heart a decent lad. Discipline and supervision will sort him out, if I may say so, sir."

"How long will he serve?"

"Until the age of 18 and thereafter for a minimum of eight years, sir."

"Thank you, Sergeant. Let the accused take the stand."

Robert Church entered the witness box and took the oath. He was trying desperately to look both innocent and chastened at the same time. However the short back and sides plus the scars on his eyebrow did not help.

"Church, do you understand the gravity of the charges and the fact that you are liable to confinement in Borstal."

The hour of rehearsal paid off. "I do, sir. But I wish to apologise for my behaviour and say it will never happen again if I am allowed to join the army."

"You assaulted three boys- why was that?"

"They tried to steal fruit from the barrow. I was helping my uncle."

"I see from the doctor's report that all three boys had to be treated in hospital and one was retained overnight."

"Yes, sir, they called me a wanker and wouldn't give the fruit back."

"The police report says these boys were bigger than you."

"A bit bigger, sir."

"How did this develop into an affray?"

"Their friends joined in and then my friends joined in and the police arrested me, sir."

The magistrate intervened. "This report implies you were the ringleader. Is it true that you have been before this court on a number of occasions for disturbing the peace and common assault, Church?"

"Yes sir, that is why I want to get away. I want to make something of myself."

"Very well, you are placed in the custody of Sergeant Parkes. Whilst I cannot make you enlist, a failure to do so will result in your appearing before me again when I shall not feel in so benevolent a mood. This case is bound over."

September 1950

Alan Barlow surveyed the scene on the platform and silently wished that the guard would blow his whistle and the journey to masculine freedom could commence, as his mother said for the umpteenth time 'How will you manage without us?' followed by 'Your father would never have agreed'. Earlier it had been 'I can't understand you wanting to leave home'.

He steadfastly maintained the sort of indifferent, manly reserve that only the sheer maleness a sixteen year old lad could achieve without drama training, as he gazed at the welter of femininity that stood there. Even the dog was a bitch; as were the three cats and two rabbits back at the house. At last the guard succumbed to his silent entreaty and the whistle blew, the engine juddered and there were more floods of tears as his Mum poured out her emotions at the loss of the last male member of the family and his three sisters joined in. Because it didn't understand the true solemnity of the occasion the bitch wagged her tail and peed on the platform as a mark of feminine weakness in the presence of true androcentric Yorkshire virility.

"I shall be OK." He started to wave.

A Sin to Tell a Lie

"You've never been alone before." His Mum wailed.

He wanted to shout 'that's why I want to be off' but he maintained his stiff upper lip, as befitted a properly reserved Yorkshireman going off into the world. After all he was only going to Chepstow; it was hardly the French Foreign Legion although he had thought several times that maybe North Africa had its attractions as an alternative because there was little in the way of warm sunny sands in Yorkshire or Chepstow. The train gathered pace as he gave one final farewell wave, breathed a sigh of relief and shut the window.

My journey had seemed endless. The prick of a clerk at the Recruiting Office in the Canterbury Drill Hall had seen fit to make out my train warrant to start at Herne Bay instead of Sturry which was only a few minutes down the road. Even when this was pointed out he refused to issue a new one on the grounds that the 'ossifer 'as already gorn' and other lame excuses. He was probably the originator of the expression 'jobsworth'. This meant I had to take a taxi at 4.30am to Herne Bay Station to catch the slow train to London. The taxi cost more than the two days pay, plus ration money, pressed into my hand after swearing my life away. Naturally there was no tip and I had my first experience of my new army life when the taxi driver muttered that I was a miserly little bastard when I failed to meet his expectation. My case was lamentably small, but even then it was nowhere near full and I had only two shillings remaining. Just for a moment it crossed my mind that I had with me everything I possessed in the whole world! Mum had cried her eyes out as I left because she knew soldiering was a hard life but the more she cried the more certain I was that I was doing the right thing. Mum was equivocal about the army as her grandfather had served for decades in the HLI but it was not quite respectable; also her father had been in France in 1916 and those terrible Huns had tried to shoot him! It was a pity really because Mum's views were coloured by what she had seen in a pre-war garrison town. She had been raised in Dover, the great Dover Castle being the home depot of several brutal Scottish regiments before the war and whose soldiery normally reduced the town's public houses to rubble each Saturday evening. Several times she warned me not to get into fights and drink! To pacify her I promised that I would not fight Scottish soldiers. As I was to find out later in life that was an extremely wise decision because the Jocks made formidable opponents – and that was just to our side.

The journey to London was slow but uneventful. Had the journey lasted any longer I may well have been the first casualty because there were no toilets or drinking water in the third class compartments. A visit to relations two years previously had prepared me for the London Underground and I arrived at Paddington with grit in my eyes, nose and mouth: thre'ppence of my precious cash reserve went on a cup of tea. I had no idea prices were so high! Even a newspaper could be had for tuppence or less. The train trundled through to Gloucester, then it was 'all change for South Wales!' with a great clanging of doors and drifting steam and smoke. A few minutes later, as that train departed, I noticed three other lads about my age, looking slightly nervous and all carrying small cases. We eyed each other but no one spoke until a porter passed by and spoke out with a laugh, "You boyo's for Beachley? The Chepstow train is running late – be ten minutes yet. You lot must be daft joining up, National Service was enough for me!"

The lads looked at me, I looked at them. I've seen less suspicion when several strange dogs meet. However in the time it took for the train to arrive we had just about managed to acknowledge each other. I remember them to this day. There was Don Lee, slightly bigger than the rest of us but calm, Don Epps who seemed confused and lost as I was and Allen Castle.

A Sin to Tell a Lie

Allen Castle was dreamily enthusiastic about the army. Strange for someone who looked as if he'd just come straight from the farm with his rosy cheeks and wild hair – which he had.

The ticket collector obviously viewed us all as potential fraudsters, crooks and hooligans. First he checked the compartment for damage, then he examined our tickets with extreme care, peering through steel rimmed glasses with a highly suspicious glare. "Why aren't you lot in uniform?" His eyes transfixed me, I was obviously the arch criminal of this gang.

"We only joined up yesterday."

"How old are you?"

"Fifteen."

"You must be out of your bleedin' mind, lad. They'll have you out in Korea fighting those fuckin'chinks before you know it."

"We're going to Beachley, to the Apprentices School."

"Aint you read Kipling, sonny." He shook his head in wonder at our foolish naivety, "Ours is not to reason why, yours is just to do as you're sodding well told until the day you die. When I got called up to do my National Service they put me in the cookhouse; couldn't cook to save my bleedin' life. I must have poisoned thousands – fuckin' thousands I tell you!"

"May I have my ticket back, please."

"Here y'are. Don't let me catch you travelling without a ticket. I keep a special watch on you lads. None of you can be trusted in my view. I bet if the truth were known you were sent here by the judge!"

The day's journey had taken place on the 4th September 1950. The memory of standing on the Herne Bay railway platform in the early morning cool remains clear. Everything I possessed in the world was either on my back or contained in a tiny cardboard case; my total value being barely three shillings and that mostly for the chemical constituent parts of my body. I *really had little idea of what lay ahead; in any case there were no guarantees! Yet at the same time I had faith in the future; I do not recall ever thinking of myself as a supreme optimist but surely that was what I had been! What we all were. How else would so many stay the course? A large dose of the optimism of youth sustained me. We are only ever given one dose; thereafter you must succumb to reality.*

Sergeant Emery, who was to be our platoon training sergeant, was a kindly dedicated soul. He said words of welcome, showed us our barrack room and told us our army number which we must never, ever forget! Said we could pick a bed and then he kindly walked us to the cookhouse. The road led us along the lines of barrack rooms that seemed unnaturally quiet and uninhabited. Being new and as yet unaware of the rhythm of the camp we did not appreciate that the older apprentices were at 'work', being fashioned into soldiers; there seemed to be no sign of life. It came as a shock when a scary voice from an unseen person called out loudly 'You'll be sorry!' I knew just what that anonymous eerie Cassandra meant a few minutes later when the cook banged some slush on my plate followed by a greasy, gristly rissole of questionable recipe and derivation. Faced with the most unappetising meal of my entire life to date I was unable to eat. The lad opposite who came from 'Livverpewl' had no such foolish inhibitions, he downed his own and mine in minutes and was looking for more. Just for the moment I held him in contempt; it was a stupid and foolish superiority that was to last at best a bare twenty four hours. After that I ate every bloody thing put in front of me and looked in vain for more. Later we spent an enjoyable evening learning how to make a bed in three different ways, the rudiments of house work including the barrack room cleaning rota, aspects of personal cleanliness, even longer absorbing all the things we must not do and how to go on 'sick parade'. This

A Sin to Tell a Lie

last one was organised so you could be marched to see the Medical Officer, even if you were unconscious. After that the evening was our own so we all went to bed exhausted. After our introductory meal I considered some may die of food poisoning but we seemed to be in rude good health, even those who had eaten double rations. Also, as we quickly found out, the NAAFI failed us as a source of dietary supplements because, like all good public schools, it was almost impossible to get served as older lads demanded and got precedence over mere 'rookies'.

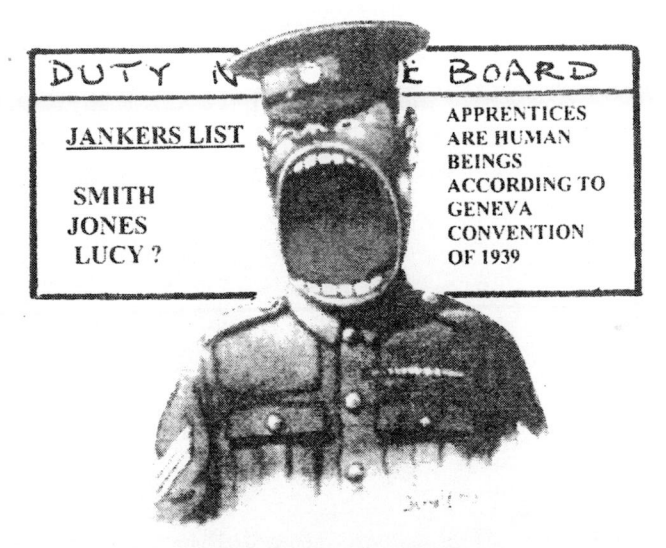

DUTY N̶ ̶E BOARD

JANKERS LIST

SMITH
JONES
LUCY ?

APPRENTICES
ARE HUMAN
BEINGS
ACCORDING TO
GENEVA
CONVENTION
OF 1939

**WAKEY, WAKEY!!
OO SED GIMME A
KISS!!!**

A Sin to Tell a Lie

I never heard 'lights out' but by God I heard the bugle sound 'reveille', accompanied by a cruel scolding NCO just a few minutes later, at the start of a cold dawn I had rarely experienced before. The room was bloody cold and we nearly died of hypothermia before learning that the first thing you do is get partly dressed and move fast.

That first morning had a surreal feel about it. We were soldiers but had no kit or uniform. We were forced into lines; oh how the army loved lines, especially straight ones, and we were marched wherever we had to go in a semblance of a squad, even though we couldn't march in step. At mid-morning a kindly, avuncular, Scottish gentleman with a tam-o'shanter on his head and striped trousers addressed us. Seeing our puzzlement Sergeant Emery had explained, "Put your feet together! Stand still and listen. This is your company commander, Captain Halford." We could tell from the crashing exact salute, his tone of voice and the deep respect therein that this Commander was someone very holy, someone to be venerated. I doubt if the Dalai Llama could have been accorded deeper respect by all his monks than we exhibited that day.

Captain Halford did not look fierce but he told us in a stern voice that we were in the army now and he replaced our parents. In fact he had complete parental control including the right to thrash the living daylights out of us if he thought fit and if that failed there was the full weight of King's Regulations to make our lives a misery – ranging from total cancellation of pay through to imprisonment. We had sold ourselves into near slavery for a few shillings a week! However, just for the moment on account of our tender years we were safe from capital punishment and the firing squad! My respect for Scottish soldiers increased because it was obvious from past experience that they cocked a snook at such trivial punishments. Captain Halford had however achieved his aim. I was not a Scottish soldier and he had frightened the life out of me. Naturally I quickly adopted the persona of a trained soldier and used my best endeavours to ensure that my misdemeanours were unobserved. The first commandment 'thou must not be caught' was duly noted. The ease with which I accepted these new morals may have troubled someone with an inelastic Christian conscience but like most young lads I quickly learnt to adapt to a more philosophical ethos to suit my new surroundings. But this was just the beginning; the wonder of many new commandments had yet to be discovered alongside the search for the holy grail known as 'extenuating circumstances'. In one respect Sergeant Emery failed; he never spelt out the new commandments though he seemed to fall back on the potential chastisements of the 'Old Testament' with some frequency to stimulate our learning processes and hold our attention. The new commandments were therefore discovered rather like the answers to 'The Times' crossword puzzles - only after due thought, observation and analysis. It came as a surprise to me that some lads could not deduce these 'Commandments' and continued to commit varying sins for which they were duly chastised and occasionally imprisoned.

A three year regimen and disciplinary cycle had started and thereafter our life was ruled by a timetable that rarely varied. We became conditioned like Dr Pavlov's dogs; the one's which drooled saliva every time a bell rang because they thought it was dinner-time. Also we quickly fell prey to the army's multiple pronged trick training technique, whereby in the first part no one dare fail as an individual because you would look a public prat! Secondly, in lieu of a real enemy, they appoint a superior rank to piss you off completely to unify the group hatred. This causes you to unite with people who in any other circumstance you would run a mile from; rather

A Sin to Tell a Lie

euphemistically termed as 'team building'. Lastly you are only allowed to speak in reply to loaded questions that are designed to make you look an utter plonker, like 'you are a fuckin' idiot, what are you?' or 'your brains are in your bollocks, where are your brains?' The replies to which must be shouted out as loud as possible so everyone within half a mile is aware of your stupid desire for self flagellation as you stridently proclaim your abasing and humiliating self assessment to the world. So began our four plus weeks of basic training to turn us into something like soldiers. We came to terms with products, often for the first time in our lives, like boot and metal polish and developed affiliations to particular cleaning materials that would last for decades. Following a long line of traditional methods I burnished the toecaps of my boots with a heated spoon followed by tins of boot polish lovingly applied with spit, to achieve a desirable glassy toecap – this took a week! Then I was rudely informed that this was required every day!! Thus ended a brief honeymoon in my search for mirror like military footwear perfection and approval.

In our stiff boots and new uniforms we paraded, marched, wheeled, turned and countermarched to the time honoured rhythm, 'left, right, left, right, left - pick'em up, pick'em up, pick'em up!' Everywhere we marched a voice would shout 'Get those arms up!' as we flailed along, our arms nearly leaving the shoulder sockets. We learnt to bang our feet together in syncopated unison and keep in step with a hundred others. The drill timing was shouted out, 'one- two, three-one!', till our voices were hoarse. It was not until much later in life we grasped the motto 'Nil Lettit Illegitimae Carborundum' (Never let the bastards grind you down) to sustain our hopes. The basic discipline and cohesion that was to rule our lives was being instilled and ingrained. It could never be totally eradicated. Looking back from the hill of old age those few

A Sin to Tell a Lie

'*Shine on, shine on harvest moon – up in the sky*
I ain't had no loving since January, February,
   June or July
Snow time ain't no time to stay outdoors and spoon,
So shine on, shine on harvest moon –

   For me and my BOOTS!'

A Sin to Tell a Lie

weeks hardly merit even a fleabite in a lifetime but as a fifteen year old they represented infinity - or was it longer!

Half way through the training I made a big mistake. It was Company morning parade and CSM Young of the KOSB's, stopped to inspect me. I had previously noted that whenever his face contorted into the semblance of a smile it meant trouble. That happened now as he peered at my face rather closely, his voice suddenly harsh. "What is that horrible mess on your chin, soldier?"

Oh, dear God, the shame; I must have forgotten to remove all my breakfast! In the stunned silence he persisted, "Speak up!"

"I dunno, Sar'nt Major."

"It's a beard, that's what it is. A hairy beard! Have you got a razor?"

Not breakfast! Oh, such relief; I smiled, "No, Sar'nt Major."

"Wipe that stupid smirk from your face, soldier! Sergeant Emery! This hairy object will report to me at 11.00 hours tomorrow, shaved and his hair properly cut. Is that clear?"

The next day, shaved and suffering the gross indignity of a 'Bing special', I was further chastened as I cleaned the office toilets spotlessly clean; while ruminating on the fact that I was totally unfit to be seen in civilised society; so perhaps it was as well that we were forbidden to leave the camp. It was also as well for me there were no young ladies present to view my situation or I fear I would have died of shame. But the days passed by and I had taken my first step towards gaining a place in the immense and glorious Pantheon of humbled and shamed recruits who never forget being humiliated by the Sergeant Major.

'Why are you hanging about outside the Gates?' asked St Peter.

'Just making sure you haven't got that bleeder, CSM Young, in there, Your Holiness'.

A Sin to Tell a Lie

'Come inside lad, he's down below – we couldn't possibly do porridge for one!'

This short interlude on fatigues was also my unwitting introduction to the subject of natural philosophy when I discerned one of the great imponderable questions of the age; This, standing alongside 'The conundrum of Hammond's indivisible numbers' in its position number 2 of observable but mathematically unproven theorems. It goes thus:- Why is it that a man cannot pee through a nine inch by nine inch hole only six inches in front of his dick without spillage?; whereas he can find a well hidden lady's love nest blindfolded in a coal hole at midnight with unerring aim! (So I am told!)

During our transition from human beings to clockwork automatons a giant aeroplane called the 'Brabazon', the oversized and ill fated Jumbo of its day, filled the sky above us doing some sort of trials over the Bristol Channel. But it was not only aeroplanes that filled the skies – we also had our share of hovering shitehawks, known affectionately to the 'Birdwatching Fraternity' as seagulls; these often hovered over our parades. Unwittingly it was an anonymous and unknown seagull that produced our first hero. This bird like others of its kind, having scavenged around the camp and the adjacent rivers, was attracted to our Saturday morning parade. Ordinary mornings were a sight to see with all their glitter and polish but Saturdays were extra special – it must have been in readiness for a Saturday parade when the Israelites were ordered to brasso their shields and blind the Philistines with powerful bolts of sunlight when they went on parade! Thus 'Bull' was sanctified in the Old Testament and was later adopted by the British Army as a form of religion. However without Biblical intervention we positively glowed with reflected light and any hand foolish enough to touch a crease was liable to need stitching. It is my belief that the seagull involved was blinded by a shaft of light from our parade whereupon it took fright and dropped a load right on poor Tommy. It spread from his hat, down his tunic to finish at his right knee. With all stoicism of the ancient Greeks a stunned Tommy remained rigidly to attention. After all he was a trained soldier, a coiled spring awaiting a command that was not given; no, he was a British Tommy and must learn to be shat upon from a great height without flinching!

The CSM was impressed and Tommy fairly glowed beneath his layer of guano as he was praised for his steadfastness on parade. He was an example to us all! Tommy was the stuff of which heroes are made, said the CSM! We would be wise to follow his example; nay, we must follow his example or we would be crapped on twice – once by the shitehawk and if observed taking sensible evasive action by an irate CSM, for moving on parade!

It took Tommy three days and two bottles of 'Dabitoff' to remove the marks. Now there's real devotion to duty and 'Stoicism' for you. While it is true that 'Dabitoff' can on occasion remove dirty marks it failed miserably to destroy the smell! But then I suppose that is why shitehawks are called shitehawks by many a soldier. Tommy was quite properly noted and marked down as NCO material but I do believe he was the first among us to achieve this recognition via rigid immobility and stoical self control.

Gradually we became accustomed to big boots and uniforms and eventually the day arrived when we were ready to take our place in the school morning parade under the watchful gaze of the awesome RSM Baker (Guards, Grenadier, large, for the use of, SIR!) – he could spot an eyeball twitch without permission at two hundred yards and read impure thoughts simultaneously, especially when these were directed at Regimental Sergeant Majors.

Seeing him stalking along a line of apprentices always reminded me of one of those hideously menacing tall machines from outer space in 'War of the Worlds'. However as time went by we developed an unspoken admiration for him. It had nothing to do with his voice of command, or his great size nor any other obvious military feature. No, it was, in modern parlance, his 'cool'. Neither Generals, the weather, irritating cock ups, etc, seemed to faze him; he had a knack of always appearing to be in control, never in a panic, an imperturbable impressive authority.

I can just imagine him on the approach to Khartoum having just marched across five hundred miles of arid pest ridden desert, his underpants full of sand, grit under his foreskin and only one tiny cup of recycled piss per man per day – and, worst of all, rankers forbidden even to spit on their boots! ....

More desolate desert stretched to the horizon and the sand shimmered in the heat. "Something is stirring out there, Sir." The RSM saluted smartly.

The Colonel lowered his binoculars, "Good God, Sergeant Major Baker! There are twenty five thousand armed and mounted blood thirsty savages rapidly advancing to our front!"

"I can see them, Sir." He studied them for a moment. "They appear to be somewhat hostile."

"Gad, Sergeant Major, we shall be overwhelmed in minutes!"

"Never fear, Sir. Ten rounds rapid followed by the bayonet should settle their hash, Sir."

"But what about afterwards?"

A Sin to Tell a Lie

"The Warrant Officers and Sergeants Mess wish to invite you to dine with us this evening, Sir. At twenty hundred hours. For the moment I think it best if you give the order to open fire, Sir, before that Fuzzywuzzy sticks his spear up your horse's ar - backside."

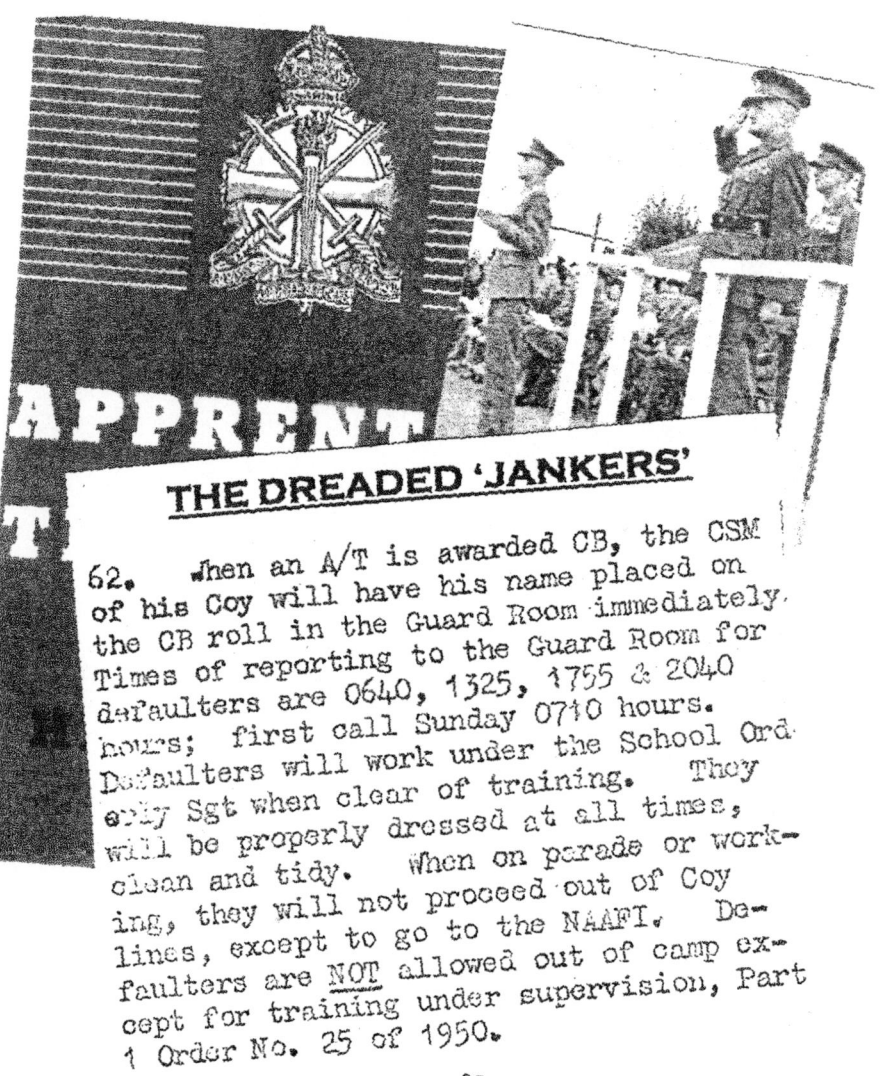

THE DREADED 'JANKERS'

62. When an A/T is awarded CB, the CSM of his Coy will have his name placed on the CB roll in the Guard Room immediately. Times of reporting to the Guard Room for defaulters are 0640, 1325, 1755 & 2040 hours; first call Sunday 0710 hours. Defaulters will work under the School Ord only Sgt when clear of training. They will be properly dressed at all times, clean and tidy. When on parade or working, they will not proceed out of Coy lines, except to go to the NAAFI. Defaulters are NOT allowed out of camp except for training under supervision, Part 1 Order No. 25 of 1950.

"I DON'T CARE WHAT THE ESCAPE COMMITTEE SAY, YOU CAN'T HAVE BOOKS ON FORGERY, TUNNELLING OR SAFE ROUTES!"

Having moulded us into the exact shape, obedience and format expected of a British soldier whereby we would on any given command advance, without a quibble or even a smidgen of disobedience, into the teeth of devastating machine gun fire from which none would return alive; the army then subjected us to detailed psychiatric and intelligence quotient assessments followed by educational and dexterity examinations so no part of our conscious or unconscious make-up, physical and mental, could be left unexamined, unexposed or unrecorded.

I remain convinced to this day that it was to see if any shred of individualism or defiance remained to be stamped out before we were unleashed to learn the fundamentals of a trade at public expense. Even then they seemed unwilling to trust the modern assessment results because following this rigorous examination we were taught the rudiments of every trade on offer to make sure that the results matched the original conclusions. It is called the 'belt and braces' selection method and of course it is a wonderful way to correlate methodologies at considerable expense. It was with some relief later in life that I learnt the simplistic sod's law method, essential to modern business – it's called 'if the prat can't do it, fire 'em!' methodology. (Very similar to Darwin's theory regarding survival.)

Luckily for the future of the army the natural resilience and scepticism of young lads ensured that the sparks of individualism and incredulity were never quite stamped out; deep down our minds were, with one or two notable exceptions, never subverted and we secretly maintained a healthy unspoken disrespect and scorn for elderly authority. The youthful mind is quite adaptable; it knows that those in command today are on their last legs, so it just bides its time! Surely it is youths' solemn and god given right to arrange and implement their own cock-ups when they are grown up and not simply repeat the mistakes of their elders!!

Rock the Boat of Life

You can't do that! Not here.
The voice sounds cross, though almost sincere
  -at least I thought it did.
My mind went blank, but then it cleared.
Why not it asked?
But questions were not required I feared.

No Entry, said the sign. Keep out of here!
A sign of authority it was clear
  -trespassers will be prosecuted.
My thoughts were stubborn I do recall.
Is that so?
But the endless barbed wire said it all.

Don't answer back, don't question me!
The finger points and wags. I am authority
  -do as you're told, we know best.
My mind rebels and searches for an answer filled with wit.
Bollocks!
Oh, how I hope that rocks the boat of life a bit.

October 1950

As I lay in the gutter bruised and shaken, my Mother's saying 'trouble never comes singly' occurred to me. One of my plates was shattered, one knee of my trousers was shredded, my jacket sleeve was filthy dirty, my head had a gash and my pride was in tatters. The plate alone was going to cost a shilling to replace!

We had been marched to the dining room for dinner as we did every weekday, several platoons very close together. On the command 'fall out' we had energetically jostled to be first in the queue. This was quite normal, nobody wanted to be last, the queues were both tedious and time wasting. In my eagerness to get ahead in the queue I failed to notice the rear assault by 'Big Geordie' as he powered his way forward. Considerably much bigger than most of us he already had the build of a good rugby prop forward, which he was destined to be, and he used it to advantage. Unfortunately for me I got in his way and was unceremoniously crashed aside.

Rob Church helped me to my unsteady feet. "You OK?"

Big Geordie looked over and shouted something harsh and unintelligible. He spoke in a foreign language that most of us couldn't understand but we usually got the gist of his meaning from the tone of his voice and his formidable facial expressions. The translation was somewhat like this – "You arseholes from one platoon had better watch out!"

"What did that big bastard say?" asked Rob.

Big Geordie raised a large fist and waved it at me, it was clear that I was being invited to place my face on it. Something that even when feeling brave I would normally decline! More abuse and scornful words were uttered on the lines of "If you want some of this come and get it!" His fist waved again.

Rob gave me his plates to hold. "That bastard is looking for a fight. Wait here." He walked over to confront Big Geordie and glared, "What did you say?"

"Ah wore sayin if won of youse won play-toon bastards wants tae fight aim'm yer man."

"Six o'clock. On the waste ground behind the huts – be there you outsize c**t!"

At six o'clock over a hundred lads assembled but it was all over in minutes as a seasoned street fighter delivered blows so fast and furiously that a dazed and confused Geordie was lying on the ground unable to retaliate. Rob stood over him his finger pointing. "Learn some manners, you Newcastle twat!"

Some 53 years after this event I met 'Big Geordie' at a reunion meeting. Was this cultured, mannered and well spoken gent the Geordie I had known? Was the smiling, welcoming bonhomie and handshake a prelude to a kick in the 'heed'? No; the Army's skill in moulding people, allied to personal ambition, had created a new George. Someone I was proud to call a friend. The blighter still owes me a shilling for that plate though!

November 1950

Going out on the town was no easy matter. The army placed many obstacles in our way. In the first place the weekly pay parade was a sham. Most of what they condescended to give us was taken up buying cleaning kit like brasso, blanco and boot polish. These were items that the army regarded as essentials whereas we tended towards egg and chip suppers in the NAAFI and trips to the town in search of the comfort of female companionship and the freedom to do exactly what we

A Sin to Tell a Lie

wanted to do for once in a while. In the second place we had to dress up as if going on Commandant's parade and then be inspected in the Guardroom by an officious and joyless Provost Corporal to determine if we were fit to be seen by the great British public that was paying for all this freedom and frivolity. Once we had passed inspection we had to sign out with a dire warning of the consequences of arriving back even one minute after ten thirty. If you were one minute late you got charged and confined to barracks, five minutes late was AWOL and meant imprisonment while being twenty minutes late meant the firing squad!

It was with some trepidation that my friend Alan Barlow and I caught the bus to Chepstow for our first taste of freedom for ten weeks. Alan was a bit of a puzzle to me; he had actually left school before enlisting and had been training to be a draughtsman, earning the princely sum of £1 per week plus some extras. Not only that but his Mum and several sisters looked after his creature comforts as well; this devoted and humble service came as naturally as life itself to a canny Yorkshireman! I regarded him as an astute man of the world. I was reassured, if anyone knew where to find the girls and how to handle them it would be Alan.

We walked up the town, then down the town, our boots clonking on the pavement; then we walked around the town before walking up and down it again. There was a distinct lack of the female form. Several of our contemporaries disappeared into the cinema facing Beaufort Square - at least it was warm in there. Not us, oh no, we were made of sterner stuff. Eventually we made our way to the Kadena Café by the Square. Perhaps we should have gone earlier but at sixpence a cup of coffee this was liable to be an expensive evening. The place was full of apprentices talking to girls; but girls who

A Sin to Tell a Lie

THE MEDIEVAL GATEWAY, CHEPSTOW

LOOKING UP AND LOOKING DOWN THE CHEPSTOW HIGH STREET.

CHEPSTOW HIGH ST LEADING DOWN TO BEAUFORT SQUARE

A Sin to Tell a Lie

seemed to be spoken for. They certainly didn't seem interested in yet another couple of lads in uniform and hobnailed boots, lashed up with a lovely blancoed belt! Besides which there wasn't even one spare female we could subject to the irresistible lure of our obvious sex appeal and chat up line. Half an hour later we stepped out into the night, our pockets lighter by a shilling each and bereft of company. That left two choices. There was the Castle Café or the fish and chip shop. Alan decided our best bet lay in the Castle Café; if that failed then it was consolation chips before we caught the bus. The café was empty so even the woman behind the counter seemed pleased to see us; she didn't even complain when we put four large teaspoons of sugar in our coffee and emptied her basin. Twenty minute later four girls crowded in with a noisy bang and loud chatter. Two quickly departed but the other two were obviously known to the women at the counter and got a free tea. Alan gave me a nod then with a sophisticated nonchalant air spoke to the girls, "D'you girls fancy a walk – share a bag of chips with us?"

I desperately wanted to warn him off. These were big girls. The smallest was as tall as us and fairly plump; the other girl was taller, plumper and bigger than we were. It did no good. The poor lad was obviously driven by overwhelming lustful desires that clouded his judgement. He was met with smiles, laughs and welcoming banter. "Ooh, are you real soldiers?" "You do look smart!" They had fine Welsh accents.

Alan grabbed hold of me and propelled me forward. "We're soldiers alright. Out on manoeuvres."

Another peel of laughter followed. "D'you hear that, Myfanwi?"

"I'm Alan." He appropriated the smaller girl. "Where d'you girls come from?"

A Sin to Tell a Lie

In the gloom of the Castle Walk I tasted the first real sizzling kiss of manhood; not unlike salt and vinegar I thought but with much greater sex appeal. She grabbed me very hard and held me tight, I had never realised a girl could be so strong. I couldn't get my arms around her but I did my best as I sank into her ample bosom. Bry-an, she crooned it in my ear, that's a lovely name. Then she washed my ear out with her tongue. I had to admit it felt nice. Her French kisses left me breathless. Despite the cool air I was soon warm all over. How old are you? Seventeen, I replied. Ooh, you're just right for me, do you like me? Course I do. Bet you say that to all the girls. Never been out with a girl like you before. Ooh, you're lovely, you are.

There is nothing like a generous woman to warm a man up - is there now?

It was only after we got back to camp that I realised my uniform would need pressing and my belt had to be re-blancoed but it was worth it. We had been in touch with the human race for a few hours. As we stepped out from the bus, going down the road towards the Guardroom to book in, I was whistling a tune quite happily and it was going to take a few days to wipe the smile from Alan's face! It was a unique occasion because I had never seen a Yorkshireman smile before; but it didn't last past morning parade!

The Dingly Dell of Delicious Delights

THE CASTLE WALK

'Put another nickel in - in the nickelodeon
all I want is having you and music, music, music!
I'd do anything for you - anything you'd want me to
all I want is kissing you and music, music, music!
Closer my dear come closer - the nicest part of any melody
is when you're dancing close to me
So put another nickel in - in the Nickelodeon
all I want is loving you and music, music, music!..........'

Christmas 1950

The remaining days to our first leave crawled by with incredible slowness. Despite the effort put into providing us with a special advance 'Christmas Dinner' there were few lads who were not looking forward to a Mum's special, allied to the expectation of wallowing in the luxurious feeling of not having to leap out of bed at reveille for a few precious days. Like most of the lads I had grown out of my civvies so I spent an uncomfortable first few days of my leave clumping around in uniform and hob-nailed boots while searching the shops for suitable items to wear. In the aftermath of WW2 and the all too prevalent restrictions and shortages that still existed, that was not a simple task. During this first leave there was a significant event as my sixteenth birthday arrived and swept by. The dawn of manhood had arrived. The 14 days leave raced by with unbelievable speed and soon the train was pulling into Chepstow Station once more. This time there were no problems with ignorant porters and sneering ticket inspectors; they could tell just by looking at us that they were dealing with highly trained and dangerous, uniformed killers all looking thoroughly pissed off at having to return to barracks just as they had began to enjoy themselves!

January 1951

"No talking in the ranks! Left, right, left!" Sergeant Emery was firm, even if his vocabulary on parade was limited. The whole company had been paraded and we were puzzled. Having right wheeled as we neared the guardroom it was obvious we were proceeding towards the main gateway. It quickly became clear that we were going to the Gymnasium when we left wheeled and were halted behind another company. We could see that those ahead of us were entering the Gym in single file but no one explained why we were here or what was happening. At last someone endeavoured to correct our ignorance. "When you enter the Gymnasium follow the instructions of the PTI. Do not stamp your boots on the floor or you'll ruin the wood! You are here for a medical inspection. Left hand file, forward."

As we walked through the door I can honestly say I had never seen so many bare arses in all my life. Long lines of boys were stood shoulder to shoulder as the Medical Officer strode along peering at their particular naked bits and pieces. As he passed by pants and trousers were raised, shirts hurriedly tucked in before the 'inspected, declared pure' were ushered to the exit. Such efficiency! Seven hundred lads inspected for unmentionable diseases in no more than twenty five minutes. I closed my eyes and thought of England. Obviously my equipment was unworthy of comment but otherwise in reasonable order; obviously it represented no danger! So it should have been. Had it been a car it could have been classified as 'Hardly Used, One Very Careful Owner'. Naturally I lived in hope; perhaps soon I would be able to advertise 'Used but Serviced Regularly by Careful Lady Driver'. A blissful thought. Optimism is truly the 'Fountain of Eternal Youth'.

In the meantime I listened to the blandishments of the Padre who was so desperate to save souls that he offered a free tea in the NAAFI for all those willing to attend classes and be confirmed. With twenty other souls at risk I volunteered; after all there was very little to do in the thirty minutes between the end of Sunday service and dinner being served. My ardour for salvation was considerably diminished when I discovered that the bargain was heavily weighted in favour of the Padre. It was ten lectures followed by one tea only! But as he reiterated many times, with considerable emphasis and fervour, the path to heaven is strewn with temptations and terrible seductive allurements. I could only hope and pray there was going to be more than one bleedin' free tea and lots of wonderful temptations somewhere along the way!

A Sin to Tell a Lie

I was still perturbed by that medical inspection though. What did the army think we did on leave? They obviously thought we had a wilder time than actually transpired. Was I missing out? What was wrong with me? My only comfort was that everyone in our lot had been dismissed as 'clean'; so I wasn't the only one not getting his share of the highly desirable but sinful life that the army seemed to think filled the world. There was a brief moment when writing home when I considered mentioning it, but commonsense prevailed. No, there was no point in worrying my mother with a description of apprentice's bare arses etc being displayed like a synchronised wave motion. She was bound to think there was something peculiar or wrong going on especially as we noted that the staff were exempt from this mass display! That is the sort of observation that can cause you to decide not to grow up because the MO obviously considered that old age must lead to a sinless and joyless existence that required no inspection; did that account for the many 'pow' faces that greeted us as we swarmed back into camp from leave?

To satisfy our lustful desires for action the CSM proudly announced that the entire Company was to participate in a knockout table tennis tournament with the winner getting a special monetary prize. This tournament would help fill the dark evenings of winter with useful purpose and temporarily divert our youthful minds away from vice. A huge sheet of paper went up with everyone's name on it – all 152 of us. This was one of those supreme and illustrious moments in the life of the Army that was destined to be entered into the annuls of major military cockups. Inevitably it only confirmed my worst fears and opinion of Scottish Sergeant Majors! With only two tables, three bats and four balls we entered into the spirit of competition. Had our dear CSM any idea of mathematical certainty he would have been able to calculate the number of games, always providing he could divide and add numbers. Mathematics was obviously not his strong point. At the end of three weeks we had not finished round one and all the balls were crushed. After the completion of the 76 first round games he declared the end was in sight; he seemed totally unaware that nearly the same number of games remained to be played! Undeterred and displaying all the finesse and determination of a bull elephant on heat he drove us to the final. I am led to believe that it is such blind courage that can drive a man to achieve superhuman feats in the face of an enemy and makes our army feared around the world. Surely some General would have underlined it as he sent the men out to face the foe. 'You're soldiers first and mathematicians second – never, never forget that men; you forget at your peril. Don't count the buggers – shoot'em!'.

Purely out of bias I did wonder if our CSM was one of those 'Jocks' my Mother said used to destroy the town of Dover on a pay night in her youth. I didn't like to ask in case he was offended. There was however a deeper seated and more worrying concern that on several occasions disturbed my dreams. One of my great grandfathers had served in a Highland Regiment. Were the seeds of self destruction rooted in my genes, impossible to eradicate? Was there even the remotest possibility that the CSM and I were distant blood relations! Surely life could not be so cruel. What if success in the realm of mathematical skill eluded me forever? Was I really destined for life in a Highland Regiment with only a draughty kilt protecting my precious personal equipment and the swirl of the bagpipes invading my eardrums and urging me towards destruction? When you are just sixteen such matters can seem important, especially if destruction arrived before the aforesaid personal equipment had been properly worn out.

A Sin to Tell a Lie

Dear Mum and Dad, phew the first six months is over! This is me with my kit off to join my new company. We are no longer the HQ rookies!!! I've grown 2" and I take size 9 boots now. Trade training proper starts on Monday and I am going to be an electrician. The older boys are very large but friendly, three of them gave me a belt each and another one gave me a pair of boots as soon as I got here. Our room NCO is a dwarf called Paddy Fahey, he's quite nice really but he can't spell.. your son, Brian.

A Sin to Tell a Lie
THE ROBOT

The School Magazine called the Robot was published twice yearly; the following data is extracted from the June 51 issue and relates to the period **Sept 50 to Feb 51.**

PRIZE WINNERS 50A

Vehicle Mechanics	W Milton, R Rumble, R Winter
Electricians	R Foster, P Baugh,
Fitters	R Day, M Kimber
Blacksmiths	R Fahey
Sheet Metal Work & Welding	R Wright
Education	D Leach, E Sandall, P Baugh

Representative Colours 50A & 50B

Boxing (full)   P Anzalucca

Boxing (Half)   R Poingdestre

NUMBERS OF QUALIFYING TRADESMEN LEAVING (48A)

Vehicle Mechanics	36
Electricians	12
Fitters	18
Blacksmiths	7
Sheet Metal Workers	<u>13</u>
Total	86

A Sin to Tell a Lie

February 1951

Early in 1951 I was struck down with flu and was whisked off to the hospital of RAF St Athan's. It proved to be nothing serious but I suppose the MO was being cautious. Not long after my return our first six months of training was completed and our group was dispersed to the main holding companies. I should have been allocated, together with my original platoon mates, to join A Company but for reasons now lost in time I was sent to join C Company instead. On the second day there I was ordered to attend the Medical Centre for a check up, with the result that I arrived back in the company lines on my own, a few minutes earlier than normal. It was too good a chance to miss. I grabbed my utensils and plates and made a rapid advance on the dining room ready for an early dinner. The anticipatory pleasure in being first in the queue was intoxicating, as well as mouth-watering!

"Stop! Where are you going?" The military training sergeant confronted me.

I skidded to a halt, "Dinner, Sergeant."

"Running is not allowed. You're early; where's your platoon?" Suspicious eyes held me transfixed to the spot.

"They're at the workshops."

"Why aren't you with them?"

"Just got back from the Medical Centre, Sergeant."

"Can't be much wrong with you if you can run!"

"The MO discharged me, M.A.D*, Sergeant."

"Is that so. Attention! About turn. Quick march."

He marched me up the road and left wheeled to the Company Office. "Halt! Left turn. Wait there!" He disappeared in the door. Several minutes later he reappeared.

* Medicine and Duty

A Sin to Tell a Lie

"The CSM will call you in, the C.O. wants a word with you." Having apprehended a military master criminal and delivered him to justice he marched off rather proudly.

Time passes slowly when a hungry belly gripes at you. Squads of apprentices passed by, the lads eagerly looking forward to their dinner but the activity quickly peaked and I was left with diminishing hope and increasing appetite. Eventually CSM Kidd looked out and stood me at ease. "The C.O. will see you in a minute, lad." He shook his head as he gazed at me, "Tch, tch!" His tongue clicked and he looked somewhat annoyed, as if he had spotted a pile of dog turds on a parade ground, before he disappeared inside.

The Orderly Corporal appeared carrying a box in one hand and papers in the other. As he tried to open the door he dropped the box and keys spilt onto the ground. He demanded I give him a hand.

At last CSM Kidd beckoned me inside to stand in the hallway; he knocked and opened the door of the holy of holies, "Shall I march him in, Sir?"

I heard the reply clearly, "No, I haven't got time now. My wife is expecting me. Give the little bugger a good telling off and say I won't have him running around like a mad hooligan; we must have discipline. Put him on fatigues to teach him a lesson."

When I got to the dining room dinner was over.

"Is there a problem, Sergeant Major?" Captain Marsden sounded irritable and he was. His wife had complained loud and very long at breakfast regarding the lack of a decent social life for officer's ladies on the Beachley peninsula. Not only that but she had demanded he recall the last time he had taken her out other than to the officer's mess with all its boring old farts. Not only that but the school band had played at the last 'do' and there hadn't been more than one tune in tune. Nor was she going to that frightful bloody bore known as the Beachley Ladies Club. If she had to sit through one more ghastly recital by some amateur singer just to please the Commandant's wife she would throw up! He had offered the local whist drive as consolation but that looked likely to rebound on him as there was a direct threat of a cessation of bedroom comforts – although it appeared he was also failing in that department as well. He was glad to go to work for a change.

CSM Kidd saluted. "Bit of trouble, Sir. Someone broke into your office during the night." The maintenance man finished scraping out the old putty from the frame to get ready for new glass.

"Someone broke into my office?" Ronnie was genuinely puzzled. "Damned cheek! What nasty little blighter did that?"

"Don't know, sir. Whoever it was broke out a pane and put in a hand to lift the latch. But I've checked your office and I don't believe anything has been touched. Rather pointless really, just silly vandalism. One of the lads having a lark I expect, Sir."

"Lark! I'll give him a lark when we catch him. Little bugger! Have you made a thorough search?"

"Yessir. Nothing appears to have been touched – none of the locks are broken. Your window was open and one pane smashed but that is all. It must have been done in the night because the Orderly Sergeant walked past at ten thirty and there was nothing wrong."

"Have you checked with the Provost Sergeant and made a report?"

"Yessir. They heard nothing."

"I will see you in ten minutes; ask around in case anyone knows anything."

A Sin to Tell a Lie

"I shall do what I can, sir but there is another problem that affects me as the Cycling Club Organiser. Twenty bicycles were booked out at the club yesterday evening – but only nineteen lads booked out at the guardroom and came back!"

"The police will fetch him back. Simply give them his name and address."

"That's the trouble, sir, I don't think the missing lad is a member and he gave a false name. The only thing I'm sure of is that he's not C Company."

"You mean the little bugger lied!"

"I'm afraid so, sir. Apparently the bike was booked out by Michael Mouse. Whoever he is, he could be half way to John O'Groats by now."

Captain Marsden was troubled as he sat at his desk; there was something wrong but he couldn't figure it out. Having convinced himself that nothing was missing he rechecked his drawer and filing cabinet again, just to be certain. Strange, even a packet of cigarettes and some loose change was untouched. Nonetheless there was still something odd. CSM Kidd had reported that a thorough search of the main office had found nothing wrong or missing; in fact Sergeant Swift was convinced that the intruder had not even entered there because the door had been locked when they arrived. Why had the mysterious intruder broken in? There was nothing to do until ten o'clock when Apprentice Sergeant Poyntz was due to discuss his tactics for an assessment of the athletic potential of the newly joined apprentices. Stop worrying he told himself as he got out the morning paper. By habit he poured some water into a glass from his carafe to take his daily 'Beecham's Pill'. Rather idly he recalled that he had never needed one during the war, enemy action had ensured his motions were fluid! As the glass reached his lips he recoiled in horror. That smell! Urine? He stared at the glass, then his treasured carafe. There was definitely a tinge to the liquid. He smelt again. He was sure. It was piss! Someone had filled his carafe with piss! Some bastard had pissed in his carafe. My God, I'll kill the sod! "Sergeant Major!"

The liquid spilt as he dropped the glass and the aroma spread. He looked at the spillage on his desk top. It had touched his upper lip so even now it clung in tiny droplets to his moustache and the ammoniac smell reached his throat. His clenched fist hammered at his desk, "Sergeant Major!"

Sergeant Swift looked up from his typewriter, "He's shouting for you, Harry. Sounds right pissed off to me."

It was rather late and the Officers Mess steward had closed the bar. Captain Marsden clutched his gin and tonic and stared morosely at the billiard table. The table resided in darkness. As he had switched on, the light the bulb had gone 'phut'. His partner, the Adjutant, was more philosophical; after all it was eleven pm and he welcomed an excuse to go home.

"The steward went home ten minutes ago, Ronnie – let's call it a night shall we."

"No dammit," he had left home after a flaming row so he had no desire to return yet. "I shall call the Guardroom and get the duty electrician out." He went into the hall to the telephone and was quickly back. "They'll call him. Now where was I? Ah, yes as I was saying. What is going to be done about the break-in to my office?"

"The Provo Sergeant has promised to send the night patrol in that direction on a more regular basis."

"Pah! Fat lot of good that will do. Why isn't the Special Investigation Department investigating?"

"Colonel Peter won't hear of it, Ronnie. Nothing was stolen; the only damage was a broken window pane. No real damage was done."

A Sin to Tell a Lie

"Some nasty bastard pissed in my carafe! Could have poisoned me! There will be fingerprints. We can get all the apprentices fingerprinted."

"Not on, old chap. After all, we would have to fingerprint everyone on the camp. It could have been staff – or it could even have been a stranger."

"So damn all will be done then?"

"Just imagine if we fingerprint all the staff and the boys. There would be an uproar – it could even get to the press. No, the Colonel is adamant."

"Our dear Colonel is too keen on making this camp into a public bloody school. Well I'll second that, as long as we bring back the cane to give all the little buggers a bloody good thrashing like they do at Eton and Harrow."

There was a knock at the door and a Sergeant peered in. "Duty electrician reporting, sir. Did you want me?" He stifled a yawn.

Ronnie glared at his watch, "You've taken your time! The bulb over the table has gone – needs a new one."

"I don't have any light bulbs, sir."

"You are the duty electrician, are you not?"

"I'm not provided with bulbs, sir. My responsibility is to deal with electrical emergencies - and my duty finished at ten thirty."

The adjutant intervened, "See what you can do, Sergeant, please. The guardroom should not have called you out."

"With your permission, sir." He took a bulb from a nearby table lamp and fitted it into the canopy; then switched it on. "There you are, sir," he saluted, "I quite agree with Captain Marsden's sentiments. If we can start by giving the lad who put a six inch nail in the fuse box in Room 45 a dozen strokes, I would be obliged, Sir!"

"I think that remark about thrashings is best forgotten, Sergeant!" The Adjutant touched his nose. "Don't you?"

"Of course, sir. I find my memory fades very quickly if I'm excused duties for a week."

CSM Kidd saluted smartly and handed over the mail, "I trust you are feeling better, sir?"

Captain Marsden returned his smile with a stern po-faced stare, uncertain whether his leg was being pulled or not, "Has your lost cyclist returned?"

"Not returned yet, sir but he's on his way back, thank goodness. I was getting quite concerned for him. My wife was worried the poor lad may be hungry."

The Captain fairly bristled, "Of course he was hungry; they're all bloody hungry. Where was he found?"

"He was discovered on the ferry from Fishguard on his way to Ireland, without a ticket naturally. Said he was going to seek asylum, silly lad. The police are holding him until the MP's arrive. The police say that he claims to have been brutally treated by the army and has made a complaint."

"Huh! Usual nonsense. Brutal treatment indeed! No doubt the Colonel will give him tea and biscuits in bed for a month as punishment. Anyway, why are you looking so pleased?"

"Well, just think of it, sir. This lad travelled all that way in only ten hours. That may be a new club record."

Captain Marsden put his head in his hands, "Sar'nt Major, this apprentice stole a bicycle, went absent without leave, stowed away on a ferry, will no doubt be charged for travelling without paying and has made gross accusations against the army! For God's sake don't make the little bugger into a hero!"

"Sorry, sir." He was about to say 'I thought he was likely to be excellent officer material' but thought better of it. "There is another matter, sir. The apprentice Sar'nt Major asks permission to hold a company dance. We can book the gymnasium for the 14th April. Sergeant Swift has offered his band at an attractive discount."

"Discount! You can tell him from me that we expect more than a bloody discount. Will there be a bar for the staff?"

"I'll arrange that with the Sergeants Mess."

"Will we sell enough tickets?"

"I'm sure we can rely on the senior group to persuade everyone to buy a ticket, sir."

"Good. Send out a strong verbal message saying that outright torture, extortion and violence will be frowned upon. Tell Sergeant Major Prosser that I shall be pleased to attend with my wife – and make sure no one wears boots. Last year that little bugger Hill was prancing around making out he was Fred Astaire, with bloody boots on! He nearly crippled my wife and he wasn't even dancing with her!"

"No boots it is, sir."

April 1951

Easter leave was but a faint fond memory, somewhat blighted by the fact that it had rained nearly every day. The Company dance was too good a chance to miss in the monotony of our current existence and I had willingly paid up my two shillings and sixpence for a ticket despite the fact it amounted to half a week's pay allowance. The fact that it was either that or suffer a compound fracture, was neither here nor there. As was made clear to me, there was no compulsion to attend as long as you made your fair contribution. But now I was here gazing in awe at the decorations and the spinning globe that scattered tiny dots of light in a twirling cascade over everything present. Even the torture rack of the wall-bars had been draped with coloured paper and balloons so they looked quite inoffensive. We often hung there like victims in a medieval dungeon if we annoyed the PTI. Sergeant Swift's little combo was playing a

A Sin to Tell a Lie

tune; a fine cheerful quickstep but as yet no one was dancing. The only thing doing business was the staff bar and that was crowded. The apprentices looked on in silent envy.

CSM Kidd passed by, holding a pint of beer and a glass of port wine, "Come on, lads. Get the ladies up." As he spoke the door opened and a crowd of girls walked in. "Go on, make them welcome."

That was when I saw her, a petite vision of loveliness, all alone and clutching her handbag as if her life depended on it.

A Sin to Tell a Lie

Had we been on a desert island for the last year we may well have rushed forward; but as it was, it only seemed like six months - so we played hard to get. Most of the girls stood along the wall opposite the band, in tight little groups, pretending not to see us while we plucked up the courage to approach them. That was when I saw her, a petit vision of loveliness, all alone and clutching her bag as if her life depended on it.

Her dirndl skirt almost reached the ground and cascaded out. She was just my height and would fit into my arms with comfortable ease. I had almost reached her when a larger and more determined mortal stepped in and grabbed her! It was an early lesson on the virtues of being decisive; as I stood there cursing myself a firm hand took my arm and a voice echoed in my ear, "Hello, Bry-an." It was Myfanwi.

"Hello."

"You don't seem pleased to see me, Bach."

I wasn't. Just to rub it in my vision of loveliness wafted past with a simpering smile on her face – but not for me. "I wasn't expecting you."

"We all came in a coach from the village. Da has a new job so we're moving to Cardiff in a few days."

"That'll be nice for you."

"You're not much of a gentleman are you – you could ask me for a dance. My Da is watching."

"Oh." I tried to look unconcerned.

"Who's that nice lad singing with the band?"

"That's Joe – Joe Jordan. He's the boy RSM. He's a friend of mine."

"You must be important, Bry-an."

I nodded agreement in a nonchalant fashion and said 'Hi Joe' as we passed by the stage but he was so busy belting out a song that he didn't hear me! Myfanwi smiled with delight.

A Sin to Tell a Lie

As she guided me around the floor to a foxtrot I contemplated my loss with several silent curses. Her mother and father watched benignly but I had a distinct feeling that my life was threatened if I didn't treat their daughter kindly. My feeling of well being had been reinforced by the half pint of beer discreetly placed by my hand when no one was watching but now I needed a pee. The music ended and the MC came to my rescue, temporarily.

'Ladies and gentlemen, there will be a short interlude then I want everyone up for the 'Gay Gordons' followed by the 'Hokey-Cokey'.

But there was no escape. However it was rather nice after the frantic backwards and forwards of the Gordons and the over enthusiastic crashing of the Hokey-Cokey, to be clasped to a warm bosom once more as the 'Speedy Quartet' put its heart and soul into a nice slow waltz.

'I'm wild again – beguiled again
a simpering, whimpering child again
bewitched, bothered and bewildered am I....

An alluring siren's voice whispered in my ear, "We could meet in the bus shelter if you want."

Couldn't sleep and wouldn't sleep
then love came and told me I shouldn't sleep
bewitched bothered and bewildered am I.

Lost my heart but what of it, she is cold I agree
She can laugh but I love it –
, although the laugh's on me........'

"Will you miss me, Bryan?"
"You know I will."
"Cardiff's not far."
"We're not allowed to go there." I looked sad and sighed convincingly. Out of the corner of my eye I saw my vision of loveliness drifting past once more; but this time she didn't look so happy, not one bit. There was hope yet.

The bell rang. At least that meant this was the last lap. My legs were leaden after three quarters of a mile. The timekeepers and the marshals scrutinised our every effort while a small group of lads shouted encouragement. This was our introduction into the mysteries of selection and rejection in the world of athletics and it was a very simple process. You were entered for every event over a period of four hours until you had either finished every event or the MO declared you dead. I dragged myself along. Despite my protests regarding my lack of prowess over a mile and my willingness to swear on oath to this effect, it made no difference. In some mysterious fashion I seemed to be running a close second! Oh God, where are the real runners! We all understood that the Company needed athletes for the coming season and the CO's desperate desire to win a shield but let's not be stupid about this; a mile is too long. It took me another hundred yards to fathom out that trailing behind me were a dozen lads putting on an act - and a slow act at that. There was only one answer, an attack of cramp! Oh! There it was, right across the chest; just in time.

The CSM sniffed as he struck out my name. "What happened there, you were doing well."
"Cramp, Sar'nt Major. Always gets me when I do a mile."

He glared at me, "Does it now, Elks? Well, we have a cure for that – it's called RT - rigorous training. Report here every weekday evening at six. We'll get you fit, laddie – or one of us will die in the attempt!"

"I'll do my best, Sar'nt Major."

"You will, lad, you will. This is the army - not a bleedin' drama school!"

The following day the rows of nets for cricket practice went up and pitches were marked out, to my great joy. Such wonderful luxury and all carefully mown. There was an abundance of kit, plenty of bats and balls; much more than I had ever seen before and the days when a lost ball meant the end of the season were over! Overnight we became a cricket academy and at every opportunity I would rush to the playing fields to practice and begrudge the sunset. Summer was here at last in all its glory and the monotony of athletics training was alleviated by the mellow sound of bat on ball.

'Heaven - I'm in heaven,
and the cares that hang around me through the week
seem to vanish like a gambler's lucky streak
when we're out together putting - bat to ball!!!...'

As my old schoolteacher used to say 'bugger the cuckoo, when you hear the first sound of leather on willow, that's proper summer, that's when life is worth living again'. He also said on occasion that it was better than malt whisky and sex but then he was a bit perverse when the mood got him; although on the matter of whisky I came to agree with him.

A Sin to Tell a Lie

May 1951

CSM Kidd saluted, "Good mornin', Sir! Sorry to interrupt you so early."

Captain Marsden gently rubbed his temples with his fingertips to ease the tension before replying. "Is the tea ready?" He sounded irritable.

"You may wish to hear my report first, sir."

"Have you discovered who it was pissed in my carafe, Sar'nt Major?" He sounded hopeful. The desire to inflict punishment on someone for his injured feelings was still strong.

"I'm afraid not but my informants are keeping their ears to the ground, sir." He thought there was no point in saying that his offer of seven and six had gone unclaimed. "It's a different matter altogether, I regret to say."

"Oh. Something important I hope."

"Yessir, very important. Early this morning, before reveille, the Provo patrol found Apprentice Brownlow stark naked and tied to a gatepost behind the dining rooms. The one by the pathway leading down to the river. It appears he had been there some hours."

Captain Marsden put his hand to his forehead again and closed his eyes, it was time for an aspirin. "I take it you mean our Brownlow? Ghastly Brownlow! Our two left legged, oversized clown called Brownlow...." He was about to say something really rude but constrained himself. Because of his size Brownlow could not be hidden when on parade so his uncoordinated efforts were readily visible, especially by a critical Commandant who prayed for and longed for precision on his parades. Every effort to get Brownlow permanently excused boots, and therefore parades, had failed.

"Brownlow it is, sir – I know his marching leaves something to be desired, sir but he has passed his first class certificate of education."

A Sin to Tell a Lie

The fingers drummed on the desk. "I know that, Sar'nt Major but there is no consolation in knowing that a future warrant officer will not be able to march in step! Where is he?"

"With the M.O. The patrol said they found him unconscious so they took him straight to the hospital."

Ronnie felt a migraine coming on. "Oh shit, that means everyone will know and we'll spend the rest of the week making out reports! Do we have any understanding of why he was tied up there?"

"Farting, sir. Apparently he can shame a polecat into submission. I'm led to believe that he farts all night long and the other lads can't take any more of it – but that is unconfirmed, sir."

Sergeant Swift put his head in the door, "Call from the M.O, sir. Could you go to the hospital when time permits, he'll be there for the next two hours."

"Thank you, Sergeant - say I'll be there in thirty minutes. Now, Sar'nt Major, what's all this nonsense about farting."

"Sorry, sir, I should have said 'breaking wind' when speaking to an officer. Apparently Brownlow is well known for it, apparently he's what I believe is called an 'an-tie-so-cial' sort. Breaks wind a great deal, especially at night. And yesterday the cookhouse served up Mulligatawny Soup at supper."

"What the hell do we do about it!"

"We need to put him in a room on his own, sir. Or there may be further trouble – even a fatality."

Captain Marsden gritted his teeth and counted to four, "Are you suggesting we promote this wind machine to apprentice sergeant so he can have a separate bunk? An apprentice who cannot march in step!"

"No, sir but we could put him in charge of the Common Room – he would only need to be a lance-corporal that way. At least he'll be able to keep decent accounts and records."

"Have you questioned the other room members?"

"Yessir, apparently they heard nothing and saw nothing."

"So I suppose they said nothing either! What have we got in that barrack room – all the relatives of the three wise bloody monkeys!"

"Tell me what happened, Brownlow." Captain Marsden said it with a distinctly chilly tone of voice designed to frighten the truth out of a devil - one of whom in his opinion he was addressing. A devil who had already broken wind at least twice, with fearsome results, since his arrival. The M.O. looked on with a deep frown, his eyes squinting as his smell buds tested the polluted atmosphere.

Brownlow shook his head as he sat to attention, "I think I must have been sleepwalking, sir."

Now it was Captain Marsden's turn to frown as he sniffed the air. "I see. You walked to the gatepost in your sleep and tied yourself to it – is that it?"

"That must be it, sir."

"Do you usually go sleepwalking without any clothing?"

"No sir, it's the first time. I think my mind must be disturbed by bad dreams. The Sar'nt Major has shouted at me and hurt my feelings several times."

Captain Marsden turned to the M.O. "Is this possible, Doctor?"

"Apart from a touch of hypothermia which can be expected there certainly does appear to be some form of psychotic alliteration allied to sleep expropriation. I consider I must keep Brownlow here for at least four to five days under observation." The M.O. still had a frown as he glanced down at Ronnie's shoes to make sure they weren't the cause of the smell.

Ronnie played his trump card. "Brownlow, do you think you could walk a few steps?" There was a nod. "Good, now walk to the end of the ward and back."

A Sin to Tell a Lie

As Brownlow walked Captain Marsden whispered to the M.O., "Do you not think that there is some deep rooted disfunctionality and irregularity in this boy's walking and behaviour? It seems to me he has singularly anarchic limbs – totally unsuited to a military life. With his psychotic disability surely a medical discharge would be appropriate, don't you think? After a sensible period of rest, that is."

The M.O's gloom lifted, "I do believe you are right, Ronnie. I shall also try a strong medication to see if we can stop the little sod farting while he is still with us."

Captain Marsden gave a hint of a smile. "Thank you Doctor, I'm sure that Brownlow is safe and secure in your capable hands. As for you Brownlow, I will see you when you are discharged to see whether you have remembered anything else."

As he walked back to his office Captain Marsden found himself humming a tune.

'Oh when the Saints – go marching in
Oh when the Saints go marching in
I want Brownlow in that number—
When the Saints go marching in.

So when the Saints go – go marching in
Through this world that's full of sin
I want Brownlow in that number –
When those Saints go marching in....'

He glanced toward heaven and looked a trifle contrite as he said a prayer. *'Forgive me Lord but I still want to get back to my regiment and please, consider this - what if I had to share a tank with Brownlow!'* He shuddered at the thought. Two apprentices marched past and saluted smartly; the salute was returned plus a hearty 'good morning', allied to a cheerful face.

As one apprentice remarked to the other, "That was Captain Marsden, wasn't it?"
"Never seen him smile before."
"Perhaps he's found out who pissed in his jam-jar."
"Nar – he's been to the M.O. Probably been told he hasn't got the clap! There's no justice is there."

On the day of the inter-company athletics meeting we had a hard fought battle with 'B' company but just lost the athletics shield. However, we had edged out 'D' Company to get second place in the meeting and the points gained gave us the consolation of being proclaimed as the 'Champion Company'. At the close of the meeting we experienced the heady delight of being called together and the whole company marching from the field, singing the song of triumph at the top of our voices.

"Cheers! Cheers! The boys are here.
What the hell do we care, what the hell do we care!
Cheers, cheers, the blacks are here,
What the hell do we care now................"

July 1951

"Roll up! Roll up! Win a pound for sixpence." Sergeant Swift did his best to get more customers. "All the proceeds go to starving children and the old soldier's home!" He was absolutely correct, the apprentices were the children and the home was where Speedy reckoned he would finish up.

The school Gymkhana was in full swing and although the crowds weren't spending pounds the steady trickle of pennies,

A Sin to Tell a Lie

threepenny bits and sixpences helped to swell the proceeds. The 'duck'em stand' was doing good business and the three lads who had volunteered for duty were in and out of the water like yoyo's. They all looked quite blue with cold despite the sunshine. Lucky for me I had managed to persuade the CSM that my arithmetic was better than my swimming so I had been 'volunteered' to help Sergeant Swift on the Lucky Numbers stall. There was no skill attached to this game – you put your money down and you lost! The Sergeant's skill at manipulating the numbers even exceeded his talent at the piano. Winners did not win as a gift from the god of luck but were timed to coincide with the need to draw a crowd or to stimulate flagging interest. Mesmerised as I was by the sorcerer's skill I initially failed to notice the clever sleight of hand taking place at the money bucket where Apprentice Grant of the senior group was operating a con of his own. As he was handed coins or he scooped them from the table, some of them were sticking to his hand before finding a way into his trouser pockets. I thought that quite clever because I was wearing uniform trousers that had no pockets but he, canny lad, was wearing civilian trousers, a privilege of his seniority. What he didn't seem to realise was that due to his greed the weight of coin was dragging down his trousers and the volume of coin made it look as if he was developing a growing hernia! He saw me watching at one point and he made gestures that conveyed his intention to flatten my nose or undertake an un-anaesthetised circumcision if I said anything. As he was much bigger than me, possessed a quick temper and was inclined to demand that lesser mortals such as myself, clean all his equipment. I remained quiet.

"Right, lads. Time to pack it in." The marshal had already called time and the crowd thinned as the events ended and the field was cleared and made ready for the Drumhead Service.

A Sin to Tell a Lie

We had had a good afternoon and the bucket was more than half full. Sergeant Swift looked pleased. "Well done you two." He looked in the bucket as he calculated, "Must be more than twelve pounds there."

Grant smiled invitingly, "Shall I take the money to the office, Sarge, and start counting up?"

Sergeant Swift smiled in return but his voice was officious and hard. "Stand to attention, Grant! Hup! Chin up – pull that stomach in now! Come on, stomach in!" He prodded and the trousers dropped dangerously lower. "You must think I was born yesterday." He shook his head sorrowfully, then he gave both pockets a hard bang and Grant gasped in pain as his bollocks got trapped. "Empty those pockets into the bucket, Grant - before your bloody trousers fall down."

A miserable Grant emptied his pockets.

"Pull the lining out – and empty the back pocket."

"That's my pay, Sarge – my own pay." His pleading brought him close to tears.

Sergeant Swift remained adamant. "Bollocks – you lost it all playing the numbers," he looked at me, "didn't he, lad? Unless of course you want to make the close acquaintance of the Provo Sergeant, Grant." An even more miserable Grant complied until his pockets were empty. "You can fall out now, Grant, so be off while the going is good." He turned to me, "You lad - you can help me take this lot back to the office."

Half an hour later I was back on the field to collect the table with two florins tucked safely in my shirt pocket for being an honest helper, whistling a tune and feeling good. There was at least another three to four shillings in bronze coinage of the realm waiting where I had trodden it into the grass under the table, awaiting discovery like buried treasure. And it wasn't many weeks to the camp dance before the senior group passed out! But before that there was the thrill of a visit to RAF

A Sin to Tell a Lie

Halton as we battled the other three schools for sporting supremacy –and no parades for three days! Small wonder I was whistling a happy tune; pennies were certainly falling from heaven and I was a lucky recipient.

'Every time it rains it rains - pennies from heaven
don't you know each cloud contains - pennies from heaven
you'll find your fortune falling - all over town
be sure that your umbrella – is upside down
change them for a packet of sunshine and flowers,
if you want the things you love – you must have showers
so if you hear it thunder - don't run under a tree
for there'll be pennies from heaven for you and me…'.

July was a time of great excitement as the senior group embarked on their final military training, donned their new battledress uniforms and with each passing out parade rehearsal we moved steadily nearer summer leave and another notch up the ladder of progress towards the day when we also would wave a fond farewell. The exuberance of the 'Senior Group' apprentices nearing the end of their time sometimes led to silly events.

Within the confines of the barrack blocks the echoing crack of a rifle shot was unmistakeable, and when it was closely followed by the whine of a ricochet everyone in C Company within 50 yards was aware of it. Passers by sought shelter and those in their barrack rooms ducked involuntarily as if expecting further action. Within minutes staff NCOs were chasing around trying to locate the culprit, while enquiring faces crowded the windows. It was obvious where the shot had

A Sin to Tell a Lie

originated, only that day the senior group had been on the live firing range. Also they were the only people issued with rifles because of the daily demands of the military training. A little later word came that someone had been arrested and put in a cell in the guardroom. With that we all relaxed - our little bit of entertainment over.

Sergeant Kenton spat out the words like a slow motion machine gun while the Colonel listened intently. Behind the accused the RSM was going almost cross-eyed as he bristled hostility and outrage.

"....on hearing the shot and ascertaining the direction I went immediately to room 28, Sir, to investigate. A junior apprentice who was not involved but close to the incident, showed me a hole in the wall and the damage in the adjacent washroom. It was obvious that a round had been fired but there were no casualties. I paraded the entire room of apprentices together with their rifles. From my inspection it was clear that the rifle belonging to Apprentice Corporal Watts had fired a round within the last few minutes. He readily admitted that he had fired the round but claimed it was an accident that occurred when he was cleaning his rifle. I placed him under close arrest and put him in the custody of the Provost Sergeant. I made a careful search with Sergeant Witlock but no other ammunition was found, sir."

"Did you deduce from the admission, and the statement made, what path this bullet followed, Sergeant?"

"I believe so, Sir. From Corporal Watts's bed there was a line of fire that went through the wall of his bunk, out through the far barrack room wall and into the adjacent washroom and toilets. There was no sign of the bullet but the lavatory wall was damaged and the occupant heard the ricochet."

"What have you to say, Corporal Watts?"

A Sin to Tell a Lie

Corporal Watts crossed his fingers. "I'm really sorry, sir. I must have left a round in my rifle after live firing on the range yesterday afternoon. When I started to clean my rifle it went off."

The RSM gave a loud sniff and his eyes looked as if he was trying to see a fly on the end of his nose.

The Colonel ignored him. "Huum! It is to your credit, Watts, that you admitted responsibility for this incident. Luckily no one was injured. You really have been rather naughty. Do you accept my punishment in this matter?"

"Yessir."

"You are reduced to the ranks. You may count yourself very lucky. March him out, Sergeant Major."

Captain Marsden looked pensive. "We were lucky there, Sar'nt Major. Bennet was too damn close for comfort. He's a ghastly little blighter but I'd rather he wasn't shot because we'd be up to our arse in paperwork."

"Yes sir. Very lucky, it missed his ear by inches."

"Just think - a few inches to the right and I should be having to explain to his parents why he got shot while sitting peacefully on the kharzi!"

"Apparently he's quite a hero among the lads, sir. After I spoke to him it was agreed that it might be better if he did not mention it to his parents. He's going to do Cookhouse Ration Stores duty for a few weeks – purely as a volunteer of course."

"You mean he actually wants to do this duty?"

"Yessir. The lad on that particular duty can – ahem! - appropriate all sorts of extras from the stock, so I'm told. Never any shortage of volunteers but I moved Bennet to the top of the roster so he will do two weeks instead of the usual one week."

"That's theft, Sar'nt Major! We can't condone theft of rations!"

A Sin to Tell a Lie

"Of course not, sir, perish the thought." He gave a knowing look. "But I do remember during the war that we valued a soldier who could liberate a few essentials – naturally I would take Bennet off this duty if you told me to, but that would give him all the time in the world to write home."

"Now you mention it, Sar'nt Major, why would a satisfied and gainfully employed volunteer want to write home? Don't forget to emphasise to him though, the therapeutic benefits of the impending four weeks summer leave. After all, it would be unkind to lose out on leave after nearly being shot, because of too much 'appropriation' – wouldn't it?"

"I'll see he understands, Sir"

She said it very shyly, looking up under demure eyelashes, "My name is Brenda. I live at Tutshill."

Thank goodness for the senior group passing out dance, I thought. The earlier object of my desire, unseen for several months, had suddenly walked in the door. I made sure that I wasn't beaten to her side; not this time, even though she protested that she didn't dance very well. What did that matter, I didn't dance very well either but the object was to get closer together – wasn't it? She fitted very nicely into my arms and smelt of roses. A heady combination. "Where do you come from?", she asked.

"Kent."

"That's a long way off. Don't you get lonely?"

I nodded with just a fine hint of sorrow mixed with resignation, designed to promote sympathy. "It can be very lonely here – but I try not to think about it." It was best to ignore the hundreds of lads all around. "That's the worst thing in being a soldier. Being so lonely." I tightened my grip while the band played on.

A Sin to Tell a Lie

She responded by putting her head on my shoulder and whispered in my ear, "I don't like being lonely either."

There was no resistance as I gathered her closer to me and the band played our tune.

'They try to tell us we're too young,
too young to really be in love,
they say that love's a word, a word we've only heard
and can't begin to know the meaning of……….'

As the Adjutant-General said after the prize giving on the Passing Out Parade Day, when addressing the school and the assembled parents:-

'... on behalf of us all I thank the Commandant for the exhibition of excellent Drill and Physical Training... Ceremonial Drill still has enormous value in the Army and is an effective way of inculcating certain characteristics for the building of soldierly virtues. Through it is learned smartness and pride ……ready to stand up to the stresses and strains when the time comes, ready to take full advantage of life's opportunities ...'

PROUD COMMANDANT'S ORDERLIES. APPRENTICES FRANK WEYMAN AND JOSEPH KINSON, C COMPANY, IN THE SUMMER OF 1951

A Sin to Tell a Lie

"How is my son doing, Sergeant Major Kidd?"

CSM Kidd crossed his fingers behind his back, "Excellent, Mr Bennet, I'm pleased to report. He has learned how to carry out a difficult duty that required absolute honesty and integrity. *(He did not get caught mis-appropriating rations)* I consider it fair to say that he has benefited enormously from this experience and has gained from that. *(He made a lot of money as well, which he will no doubt squander on wine, women and song)* He displays all the characteristics needed for a successful army career. *(He is adept at lying and covering his tracks)* Also he is becoming the sort of soldier that I value, he'll make a fine sergeant major one of these days. *(He knows how to keep his mouth shut and get a job done even though his C.O. is a p***t)*"

"I'm so glad to hear that, Sergeant Major." Mr Bennet sighed with relief, "You know, in my day so many soldiers were simply cunning thieves and liars." Then he brightened up. "However, after listening to you and that nice General who spoke at the prize giving, I can see that the army is in safe hands and still retains the good old fashioned and proper virtues of discipline and service."

"Kind of you to say, sir."

"I do have a slight worry. It appears that Gordon spends a great deal of time associating with girls. I've told him he must buckle down and stop singing that silly song about 'Young Love', I really can't understand how the youths of today can listen to such twaddle, especially when it is sung by a middle-aged man called Jimmy Young!"

"You mean the song 'Too Young', sir. No need to worry, we rarely let them out so they have to put all their energy into becoming soldier tradesmen rather than silly gigolos."

Mrs Bennet smiled and nodded agreement as she wondered if she could persuade her husband to join, "Very gratifying, Sergeant Major. And I'm thrilled - absolutely thrilled with this gift from my son." She held out a thin brass necklace chain, from which was suspended a spent and misshapen 303 bullet. "Gordon tells me he made this with his own hands in the workshop. I shall treasure it always – but I do hope you don't let our boys play with nasty guns. They can be so dangerous in the hands of young men."

There was an eerie quiet and stillness about the place. Thank God for that thought Ronnie Marsden as he lit a fag and relaxed while Sergeant Swift had delivered a decent cup of tea and a celebratory biscuit. The last busload of apprentices had left for the railway station an hour ago. Nearly four weeks of peaceful bliss unpopulated by crass youths stretched ahead of him. He was even in good odour with his wife as he'd promised to take her to Bournemouth for a week. For the moment though a nice quiet day remained in prospect so he could complete a bit of admin before getting away. Already the sun was shining and the weather forecast was promising. There was a tentative knock at the door.
"Come in."
Sergeant Kenton put his head in. "May I speak, sir?"
"Come in, don't stand in the doorway."
"Don't like to trouble you, sir but CSM Kidd is with the RSM. Sergeant Swift thought I should let you know immediately."
Ronnie felt the hair rising on the back of his neck, "Let me know what?"
"Someone has defaced the outside walls of the barrack rooms with rude words. It can be seen quite clearly from the road. The paint is wet so it must have been done this morning."
Ronnie could sense the prospect of a blissful day ebbing away. The barrack rooms had only just been redecorated a month ago. Before he could reply Sergeant Swift looked in, "The CSM has phoned, sir. Apparently there is trouble in

A Sin to Tell a Lie

Chepstow and he has to go there with the RSM immediately. As the 8-47 for Severn Tunnel pulled out of the station hundreds of bags of haversack rations were tossed out of the train windows. Also hundreds of bags are floating down the River Wye from an earlier train going to Gloucester. You will recall we had the bags marked by Company for easy collection. It seems there are a lot of bags marked 'C' with some additions. The Colonel is hopping mad."

Ronnie felt for his packet of 'Rennies'. Oh shit!

Colonel Peter seemed remarkably sanguine considering the taut message received from the GWR Track Maintenance Manager. "I'm afraid the lads have been - well - laddish, don't you think?" he looked enquiringly around the table.

"No great harm seems to have been done, Colonel," volunteered Major Nash.

Ronnie tried to keep his look of annoyance from showing. Sanctimonious bastard, he thought, just because B company appeared to be the minor culprits. "I shall check the travel warrants to see who was travelling on that train," he volunteered rather than be overshadowed.

The Colonel's lips pursed in thought, "The RSM mentioned that even the gulls wouldn't eat the rations discarded. He is concerned that the standard may have been poor. Apparently these rations were made up yesterday evening."

"That's no excuse for improper conduct, Colonel."

"Still, it may be better to do a 'Nelson touch', what. Turn a blind eye. No, I think it best to put it behind us – we don't want it to become a tradition, do we! I trust you will enjoy the break, gentlemen, and come back revitalised and enthusiastic ready for the new term. Don't forget, a new bunch of lads are on their way shortly. I expect you're all looking forward to that."

A Sin to Tell a Lie

Ronnie chanced his luck, "We're very lucky Sir – what with all the fighting in Korea and troubles in the colonies."

"That reminds me Ronnie. I think we had better put more emphasis on boxing skills; yes indeed, it may be best to build up their martial spirits and encourage a war-like attitude. Perhaps you and CSM Kidd can give them another demonstration – before you become too old for active service, eh."

"Did I hear right?" Speedy looked aghast at Harry.

Harry checked to ensure the C.O. had gone. "If he thinks I'm going back in the ring again he's fuckin' mistaken. Unless I put a horseshoe in my glove."

"He has gone a bit...." Speedy tapped his head sorrowfully.

"Don't mention this to my Missus, she'll go balmy."

"You're safe there, old chum. By the way, did you hear the one about the duffed up old boxer?"

"How does it go?"

"Like this; there was this poor old puggled boxer, he'd lost match after match after match but he kept on at his manager to find him a suitable opponent he could beat. It's no good said the manager, you're washed up. I wanna fight wid der Canary Kid, he replied, get me a fight wid der Canary Kid; everyone beats der Canary Kid! Don't be a c**t said the manager, you are the Canary Kid!"

"Are you calling me yellow?"

"No, I'm trying to say don't be a c**t!"

A Sin to Tell a Lie
THE ROBOT

The following data was extracted from the December 1951 issue, Vol 60 and relates to the period **Feb 51 to Sept 51.**

PRIZE WINNERS 50B

Vehicle Mechanics	A Basset, M Buckland, J Harrington M Francis, J Old, D Lee
Electricians	H Finnamore, M Medhurst, R Rowell
Fitters	R Sirett, P Wallis, J Wildish
Sheet Metal Workers	M Spinks
Blacksmiths	D Birchall
Welders	A George
Education	H Finnamore, F Cresswell, R Rowell R Wooton

Representative Colours. 50A & 50B

Full Colours	R Commins (Athletics)
Half Colours	P Anzalucca, D Leswell, A Burden (Athletics), R Lee, R Maisey, R Freeman, G Ninnis, J Overend (Rugby)

Monmouth County Athletics Championships

Youths Javelin	1st	B Elks
Youths 110 hurdles	1st	R Commins

NUMBERS OF QALIFYING TRADESMEN PASSING OUT (48B)

Vehicle Mechanics	51
Electricians	17
Fitters	23
Blacksmiths	9
Sheet Metal Workers	<u>18</u>
Total	118

Disbandment of 'A' Company. On the return from summer leave, 'A' Company was disbanded and the apprentices allocated to the remaining three companies.

September 1951

He was Welsh so he answered to the name of Taff, also his name was Alfred so some called him Alfie. He was undersize so some called him Tiny – it was that matter of size which was his undoing! Apprentice Mathlin was very well liked but he had been undersized on the day of enlisting. Most lads thrived on plenty of exercise and a decent diet. Not poor Tiny: he was like Peter Pan it seemed, destined to remain 14 for the rest of his life, except of course that he couldn't fly! Tiny, aided by his mates and staff unwilling to believe they could not perform miracles, tried to grow. 'Get some more meat down you lad!' 'Try this new exercise.' He ate, he tried, and he persevered – to no avail. Now it was time to go! We were not asked for our opinion for otherwise he would have certainly stayed. Several lads tried to say he was lucky to be leaving but he steadfastly refused such consolation. The poor soul looked pathetic in his combination of crumpled civvies and army issue hobnailed boots. There was a tear in his eye as he walked through the lines, trying desperately to hold his head up and mutely acknowledging each farewell. It made me realise how far we had come in a year - and that the loss of a comrade could hurt. He was I believe, our first real casualty.

It is now 56 years on as I sit here reading his discharge details. His home address, unknown to me years ago, hit me hard and made me sad. We had sent him back to a small Welsh township in a coal mining valley not far from Tredegar; from which he had wrenched himself in the hope of a better life. From personal experience I know what a cruel and depressing place it was, with a river that ran black from coal washings. I spent two miserable years there as an evacuee early in WW2. Surely we must have been together in the same small infant's school back in those days.

A Sin to Tell a Lie

Tiny had not wanted to leave but looking back it often seems odd to me that the Army acted as if, left to our own devices, we would immediately abscond or defy all orders. An odd boy may have volunteered to leave but that was not true of the vast majority in whom had been bred an expectation of future travel, advancement and adult enjoyment. Today we were at school so we accepted some restrictions but we had no doubt that the coming world was our oyster!

"STOP 'ANGING ABOUT, LAD!!"

October 1951

Sergeant Swift could not believe his ears. Yes, he had heard it! There was a humming sound not unlike the purring of a big, contented fat cat emanating from the Company Commander's Office; good God he thought, he is humming a tune not unlike 'Happy Days are Here Again!'. "Can you hear that, Harry?"
CSM Kidd's eyebrows lifted in surprise. "D'you reckon he's been at the bottle?"
"Damned if I know! Never heard him sound so happy since Brownlow fell off the lorry taking him to the railway station when he was discharged."

Ronnie leaned back and gazed serenely at the newspaper. It only confirmed what he already knew but it confirmed it in bold precise capitals – the absolute, inescapable, irrefutable truth. Good old Winnie was back in power! Those miserable, peace-loving upstarts called socialists had got their well deserved comeuppance. No more arse licking sycophants toadying up to these damn foreigners. No sir, no! It would be gunboats and cold steel from today; and a boot up the arse for good measure! He almost felt like singing out loud 'Winston Churchill, I love you'. There would be no more foreign bastards out there tweaking the lion's nose and getting away with it. "Sergeant Swift! A cuppa tea, please – and two large sugars." He rubbed his hands in glee because life was worth loving again.

'Happy days are here again
the skies above are clear again
so let's sing a song of cheer again
happy days are here again................'

A Sin to Tell a Lie

Only a few days previous Captain Marsden had noted, with suppressed glee and escalating hope, the newspaper reports that the Egyptian Government had renounced the Suez Canal Treaty. Gad, sir, the ghastly bloody natives are turning bolshie; what is the world coming to! Where will it all end? As he had sipped his morning cup of tea he could feel his patriotic fervour rising as he read the newspaper headlines proclaiming the latest insult to the British Empire. British troops had had to take control of the Suez Canal before it dissolved into chaos and dastardly foreigners attacked more British citizens enjoying life in the sunshine. There was no mention of the need for more tanks to crush these barefooted rioters but Ronnie felt confident that it was only a matter of days before the call came to return to his regiment and put the jolly old goggles on once more. Goodbye Beachley and the bloody rain; hello Alexandria and warm Mediterranean sunshine. There was no doubt about it, while he was sat here plotting the winning of the champion company trophy via the best barrack room competition, the Empire was disintegrating. Worse still he was incarcerated on the edge of nowhere and commanded by a colonel who so far simply had not wanted to understand the obvious perils the country faced by keeping real soldiers from their duty. But now the situation was clear, his presence was demanded or else the country would fall into disrepute! Confidently he had reached for the phone. "The Adjutant please….Tommy, Ronnie here…..what do you mean you were expecting me to call five minutes ago...Oh…..I see…..You're certain the Colonel won't see me…..he made a special point of mentioning it…..right. There *is* going to be a war…..what do you mean, wishful thinking…..what if I put it in writing……that's a bit rude!" Reluctantly he had hung up. Bollocks!

Speedy glanced across to where the CSM was listing the defaulters. "He's at it again. Singing that daft song!"

The CSM's head didn't lift. "I know. I believe in polite circles it's called 'pissing into the wind'."

Speedy shook his head, "I can't understand it. We have a nice little number here. Better than Eton really, cos if the lads step out of line we can stop their pay and stick'em in the Guardroom!"

"You're a hard man, Speedy – just because one of them has wrote to the Tax Office reporting you for not declaring your band money"

"Jesus! Who the fuck has done that! What bastard...."

"Calm down – calm down. Just pulling your leg."

"Just pulling my leg! You could have given me bleedin' heart failure. Put – the – kettle on for gawd sake!"

November 1951.

The Colonel looked disappointed, a little sad even, as if he'd just been told the real odds against winning the football pools; while the Company Commanders who were sat around the table looked puzzled. No one spoke. In the prevailing silence only two things could be heard. One was the horizontal rain driving into the nearby window, the other was the gentle tick-tock of the old but official grandfather clock that the Colonel retained to give his office extra gravitas. Ronnie Marsden just wished that something would happen to get the proceedings under way. He felt somewhat uncomfortable as rain had dripped down his neck, soaked his collar and shirt that now felt clammy and cold as it stuck to his skin. It served him right for wearing a beret but then you couldn't wear a service hat in a tank; he inwardly sighed at the thought, his tank was so far away. Every now and then the Colonel glanced at the pile of

A Sin to Tell a Lie

papers on his desk and drummed his right hand fingers on the table top as if to release tension. But it did no good because the lines on his forehead deepened rather than disappearing. At last he looked around the table and spoke.

"Good afternoon, gentleman – well it would be if the rain were to stop. No doubt you are wondering why I have called this meeting – this special meeting." There was silence because everyone guessed that the statement was simply rhetorical, not a question. He pointed to the papers. "Something rather unusual and disturbing has been brought to my attention. Something regrettably serious – and worrying."

Ronnie felt a suppressed but small surge of elation, no doubt the school was to be closed and a new tank awaited him. Only yesterday the news confirmed the landing of more troops in Egypt; they were sure to need armoured support! With a great effort he managed to subdue his wild hopes and remained straight faced and soberly supportive of his colonel in his hour of need just in case his hope wasn't realised.

The drumming fingers stopped and a hand waved over the papers. "Over the last week a covert operation has had to be mounted, I regret to say. Originally a night patrol noted an odd occurrence when passing the quarters housing the female NAAFI staff. To cut a rather long and disheartening report short the gist of it is this. One of the senior apprentice NCO's has been seen entering these quarters late at night and leaving early in the morning over a period of several weeks. Latterly I took it on myself to speak to the apprentice concerned and he confirmed my view that a serious relationship had been formed that he does not wish to terminate."

The B Company Commander was deeply affronted. "Surely this soldier should be on a charge, Sir. The quarters mentioned are designated as out of bounds!"

"There is a sign to that effect but it has no legal significance - so I'm advised by the legal people at District. Also it is within the camp bounds and both the apprentice and the woman concerned are over eighteen. Although moral strictures may be voiced the view is that we cannot enforce a ban on them meeting."

"What does the NAAFI hierarchy say, Sir." Ronnie tried to sound supportive.

"The local manageress refuses to discipline the girl but she has asked her to volunteer to move to the barracks at Cardiff – so far she has refused. The manager feels that we should take action, as both the NAAFI and the adjacent quarters are actually War Department property. I can and will issue a local enforcement order regarding entry but it cannot be made retrospective. Our dilemma is this, gentlemen. On the one hand we have a very promising apprentice close to the end of his time here and whose performance has not deteriorated or fallen in any way, someone I believe we all consider to be a future leader while on the other hand we have an example that I feel is unacceptable within the context of a school and the upholding of moral standards that we must support in our role and obligation as de-facto parents. Your views please."

"Whilst I accept you may not be able to take retrospective disciplinary action, sir, surely this soldier must be discharged immediately. And if not now then most certainly if he is caught entering those quarters again!" The D Company Commander was horrified, "This is a terrible example for the younger apprentices; we simply cannot condone it. I mean, sir, - my God! – flagrant sex on the camp…what is…..." His voice tailed off as he was overcome with disgust.

"Yes, but………"

Sergeant Swift glanced out of the window at the rain. "D'you fancy a cuppa, Harry? Bloody miserable afternoon."

"Don't mind if I do," CSM Kidd glanced at his watch, "D'you reckon the C.O. will get back before five?"

"Naw. They'll be chewing the fat over this apprentice giving that NAAFI bint a good rogering. Fancy him admitting it; silly beggar! He should have said they were having prayer and bible readings or discussing politics."

"That's a bit unfair, Speedy. We must look after the welfare of these lads committed to our care."

"Bollocks! We're running a bleedin' great stud farm with no heifers, that's what the trouble is. We'll have to put more bromide in the tea. Look at that little bugger Elks at the last dance. Spent half the evening looking down that girl's dress and the other half camped out in the bloody bus shelter with her. Bloody disgraceful."

"You forget, Speedy, we had our time during the blackout. Bloody marvellous it was. Of course everything was rationed except nookey!"

A dreamy look enveloped Speedy as he remembered the good old days and he sighed. "You're only bloody right. By the way, how did they catch this lad at the NAAFI? Surely he wasn't stupid enough to leave as a patrol was passing by, was he?"

"Course not; we've trained them better than that. No, the Provo Sergeant is knocking off the manageress. Just as the lad was leaving who should walk out of a nearby bedroom but good old Henry, stark bollock naked. Good mornin' Sarge, said our lad, you're a bit cheeky this morning."

"Why did Henry report him?"

"He didn't. They reckon it was the manageress sent a note to the RSM - she wants to get the girl out."

"Shame that. That girl is the only decent looking female on the camp."

"I'm told that the Colonel had three meetings with the Padre last week."

"What the heck for?" Speedy put more paper in the typewriter.

"Probably praying for divine guidance. The RSM reckons that the Padre said we should have more church parades and include sex education in the curriculum instead of letting the lads read Hank Jansen's. Silly blighter, I bet the lads could give the Padre lessons concerning sex. But, give the old man credit, he said the lads obviously knew enough about that and it would be better spending more time on map reading and the virtues of abstinence. Unless of course the Padre was willing to work a seven day week which he refused."

"Good for him, everyone deserves a day for sinning, even the Padre! What will happen to the lad?"

"As long as he doesn't get caught again, nothing - and if he does get caught we've failed."

Speedy sighed with a degree of longing in his voice, "God, I wish I was eighteen once more - and could get it to stand up straight again every day!"

"You don't reckon your Missus is putting bromide in your tea do yer?"

"Naw – it's the other way round these days!"

"What do you want!?!" The tone was hostile, the look penetrating and the attitude belligerent. Andy Cultrop, civilian storeman, grade B(Temp) and late Acting Corporal of the Royal Lancashire Regiment was about to lock up. He had opened the yard for the requisite forty minutes and it was now two minutes into his delayed tea-break, he considered; besides which the temperature was freezing, the wind icy and he was right pissed off at having to do this duty because that bastard Haynes had called in sick. Sick my arse, he had muttered to himself several times, he can't take his drink any more and the weather forecast of snow had done for him. If only an ungrateful country had given him a half decent pension, Cultrop told himself, he could have opened a little corner shop and flogged fags and papers but no, he had to exist on a pittance and work for a bleedin' living. "I said, what do you want?"

The platoon of apprentices had halted right in the gateway of the coalyard. The apprentice NCO in charge stepped forward, "D Company coal detail, Mr Cultrop. I was instructed to collect our coal ration."

"Have you now. You're too late." He tried to wave them away.

"It's only two minutes to twelve - sir." The NCO tried politeness.

"Don't matter. All the coal has been issued. Come back next Saturday."

The NCO stood his ground. "We've had no coal."

Andy opened his ledger and sniffed aloud. "Look. Ninety tubs have been issued. Ninety tubs were authorised –that's yer lot!"

"Who took our coal?"

"I don't know who had your coal but it's been collected and signed out."

"But you must have seen who took it."

"You all look the same to me. All I know is that ninety tubs were delivered, ninety were filled, signed for and taken away."

"I shall have to report this immediately."

"You do that sonny Jim because I'm going for a cuppa."

"Are you some kind of asshole, Cultrop?" The Quartermaster glared at him. "Fancy sending an official detail away with no fuel in this weather."

Cultrop glared back, "Let me remind you, Quartermaster; I'm not in the bloody army anymore and I resent what you have just said. I shall certainly have to make this a union matter."

"You and your effing unions will ruin this country! Are you certain that ninety tubs were taken away. The D Company C.O. is livid."

A Sin to Tell a Lie

Andy Cultrop opened the ledger and checked again. "All signed for. I made sure every tub filled was weighed and recorded."

"Half of these signatures are illegible."

"They're only boys, Quartermaster, what do you expect?"

"Don't you realise that if this was Colditz then nine tenths would have escaped before now and those left would be running the fuckin' place! They don't miss a trick – you must keep your wits about you." He was about to add 'always assuming you have any' but thought better of it. "You will have to go back to the yard and issue a company allocation; then look around to see what has happened."

"I clock out in five minutes."

"You will not leave until this is done."

"I shall want three hours overtime at double time."

"Two hours."

"Agreed." Cultrop sniffed disdainfully as he thought to himself, I'd have done it for nothing but you called me a rude name. As he marched down the road, he still marched rather than walk, his brain was in overdrive. He knew that only ninety tubs in total were distributed to B, C and D companies but after filling ninety tubs a new detail had turned up with another thirty empty tubs. So had a previous lot marched off and come back directly with emptied tubs for a second lot? But was that another company or was it D Company? There was only one thing he was certain of, the new boys in H.Q. Company could not be involved; their coal had been delivered direct yesterday.

Even after marching back via the barrack rooms and checking and counting everything, there was nothing amiss! There was no evidence of extra coal anywhere. It had simply vanished. Bollocks, he thought, let's go for a pint and spend a shilling of my overtime pay.

A Sin to Tell a Lie

(There is a prize for the person who solves this con, except for the two apprentices who planned it, they will be pleased to know that the statute of limitations now applies – written solutions to the author please, not to exceed 500 words and please, a £20 note for processing costs.)

It was a cold, cold winter's evening and we had kept each other warm in the deep doorway, around the corner from the fish and chip shop. She was the new light of my short life. I would like to have met her every day but a mean spirited attitude to army pay precluded any such frequent contact. It was once a week, twice at most, and think yourself lucky. Even at this moment there was probably some publicity seeking prat in Parliament preaching the virtues of low pay and short rations to keep the licentious soldiery in check. Unfortunately for me the retentive attraction of her warm body, fervent embrace and kisses allied to the fact that the bus driver wanted to get home as soon as possible meant that the last bus back to camp was just disappearing down the road as I turned the corner to reach the bus stop! There was no alternative. It was step out at the quick march, down towards the castle and over the bridge followed by the grinding ascent up the hillside – then step out lively through Sedbury because the minutes were ticking away and that nasty Provo, Lance Corporal Gilbert, was waiting to add my name to the list of absentees. A lively tune helped to maintain the momentum ....

'Sparrow in the treetop, sparrow in the treetop
Though he loves his mate.
Sparrow in the treetop, sparrow in the treetop
Scared of going home because it's too darn late!

Don't look at me sweetheart with scorn in your eyes
Been out all night, gonna tell you no lies

A Sin to Tell a Lie

Stopped in one place, heard them singing a song
Like a lonely sparrow, I started singing along

Sparrow in the treetop, sparrow in the treetop
Though he loves his mate………………………...,

The beady eye transfixed me as the pencil poised over the book, "You're just in time!" He sounded disappointed but his look said 'I'll get you next time!'

'OUR FATHER, CAN YOU PLEASE ARRANGE FOR CORPORAL GILBERT'S MOTHER AND FATHER TO BE MARRIED. IF YOU DO THIS I PROMISE I WILL MAKE THE SUPREME SACRIFICE AND JOIN THE PADRE'S CONFIRMATION CLASS.

February 1952

The February of 1952 was a sorrowful time. No sooner had the passing out parade taken place on the 5th February than on the very next day came news that King George had died and the nation went into mourning. Young as we were I think everyone thought well of him and we were no exception. We had grown up in war and this King had stood beside us through the good and bad days, the times of worry and the few days of rejoicing. He was a widely loved and respected man. There was some general talk of an Elizabethan Age to come but grief comes first, hope is a slow burning fire. We practised the 'Remove Hats!' so on the 8th February we cheered our new Queen in proper military style on an 'Accession Parade.

The Proclamation

Whereas it has pleased Almighty God to call to His mercy our late Sovereign Lord King George VI of blessed and glorious memory by whose decease the Crown is solely and rightfully came to the high and mighty Princess Elizabeth Alexandra Mary;
We therefore the Lords Spiritual and Temporal of the Realm being here assisted with these his Late Majesty's Privy Council with other representatives of the Commonwealth with other principal gentlemen of quality with the Lord Mayor, aldermen and citizens of London do now with one voice and consent of tongue and heart publish and proclaim that the high and mighty Princess Elizabeth Alexandra Mary is now by the death of our late Sovereign of happy memory become Queen of this Realm and of her other realms and territories, Head of the Commonwealth, Defender of the Faith to whom her lieges do acknowledge all faith and constant obedience with hearty and humble affection

A Sin to Tell a Lie

beseeching God by whom all kings and queens do reign to bless the Royal Elizabeth 11 with long and happy years to reign over us.

God Save the Queen.

As we mourned, the New York Times speaking for America, said we as a nation must seek a 'new place in the sun'. On that day there was a flurry of snow here and in America nine members of the National Association for the Advancement of Coloured Peoples were arrested for attempting to gain entry for negro children to an all-white school.

At 2pm on the 15th February we stood with silence with bare heads as the King was buried at Westminster, it was reported that the whole nation and even the heart of London fell utterly silent. On the following Sunday we attended a memorial service in the school church.

Before that though, on the Saturday, we read in the newspapers, and saw photographs, of the King's 'last sad journey'. The papers were our main source of news and the pictures shown were perhaps the last great display of photographic newspaper imagery we saw before the might of television invaded all our lives.

Before the memorial service the following address from the Queen was posted;

' I wish, on succeeding to the Throne, to address a message to all ranks of my army, thanking them for the notable services they rendered to my beloved father during his reign and assuring them of my confidence in their loyalty and efficiency.

Devotion to duty, a good humoured acceptance of hardship when necessary, and an undefeatable endurance in adversity are the characteristics of the military forces which have brought us victory in war and security in peace.

I know I can rely upon them to respond to any call upon their allegiance with the same competence and enthusiasm with which they served my father.

I shall always take a close personal interest in all that concerns their welfare and efficiency.'

We have a new Queen; Her Majesty Queen Elizabeth 11

A Sin to Tell a Lie

The reviewing Major General, who had spoken at the Passing Out Parade 'prize giving' on the 6th February, was most flattering of our abilities. He told us that in time we might eventually, if we improved, reach the rank of Sergeant. Also we must remember that men are more important than machines and we must learn the way of leadership, smartness and responsibility through drill and more drill. Also we were very sheltered in the school and we must brace ourselves to meet a disappointing world.

Earlier he had emphasised the virtues of discipline. To have high morale we must have good discipline and we must discipline ourselves. We must learn to do things we didn't like and respond to orders immediately, without question. At the same time he was heartened to see we had responded to military training. He was convinced that there were some men of first class material in our country and when we were put into a good unit and learnt how to work hard the goodness in us would be brought out!

I was so pleased as I listened to him for this illuminating glimpse of our place in the army of the future; under the leadership of a General who plainly considered that we may, with considerable training and hard work, one day find a place in the gun fodder regime he obviously viewed as a necessary adjunct to his generalship! Only my great discipline prevented me from instantly throwing myself at his feet and begging for an immediate order to advance on the enemy guns – or, after more mature consideration, to petition for his retirement.

SCHOOL FOOTBALL TEAM, 1951/52

A Sin to Tell a Lie
THE ROBOT

The following data was extracted from the June 1952 copy, Vol 61, and relates to the period Sept **1951 to Feb 1952.**

PRIZE WINNERS 50A

Vehicle Mechanics	J Hardy, D Boycott, A Appleton, P Mason
Electricians	P Webb, P Baugh
Fitters	A Weyman, M Kimber
Blacksmiths	B Banyard
Sheet Metal Workers	J Bright
Education	M Beresford, P Baugh, A Morris

REPRESENTATIVE COLOURS, 50A & 50B

Full	P Mason, B Masters, W Dallas (Football)
Half	D Birchall, R Clough, M Tostevin, A Burden (Football)

FIRST CLASS CERTIFICATE OF EDUCATION

D Leach, R Taylor

NUMBERS OF QUALIFIED TRADESMEN PASSING OUT, 49A

Vehicle Mechanics	37
Electricians	5
Control Equipment Electricians	3 *
Fitters	10
Sheet Metal Workers	8
Blacksmiths	1
TOTAL	64

* The first in the history of the school. (The last would depart in Aug 1957)

June 1952.

Sergeant Swift perused his notes; as the organiser of the 'Mess Shoot' he intended that it should be well prepared and run, as well as being a lucrative source of personal income. His train of thought was interrupted as CSM Kidd thundered through the door and threw his pace stick down. "I've got another lot for your fatigues list! That sod Elks is the cause."

Speedy lifted his head and squinted, "Oh – what's he done?"

"He was moving on parade when he should have been still. I said to him 'Keep still! Have you got haemorrhoids?' He said 'No Sar'nt Major, I've got asteroids'. So I said to him 'You must have haemorrhoids. I've got haemorrhoids so I know what haemorrhoids are – don't you know the difference between asteroids and haemorrhoids?'"

"Is that why he's on the fatigues list?"

"No. It was when he replied 'Yes, asteroids attach themselves to heavenly bodies while haemorrhoids attach themselves to arseholes.'"

"Oh, I see," said Speedy "He should have said, 'Yes, Sar'nt Major, asteroids .....'"

The RSM looked down from his lofty height. Despite the fine summer day and clear sky he was the only person present not in shirt sleeve order. "Those odds are a trifle mean, Sergeant Swift." His lower lip jutted out disdainfully and under the peak of his cap his eyes narrowed in a disconcerting fashion, "Damned mean!"

Sergeant Swift's chalk hovered over the tote board. "Who do you want to bet on, Sar'nt Major? Perhaps I can accommodate you."

There was a loud sniff. "Even money on Sergeant Riley! Are you building a pension fund by any chance?"

A Sin to Tell a Lie

It was Speedy's turn to sniff in disdain, "Chance would be a fine thing. Riley won last year and he's leading now – odds ought to be 2 to 3 on, by rights."

The RSM gave a baleful look and went to walk away.

Fearing his card was about to be marked Speedy wisely made an offer. "As it's you, Sar'nt Major I'll give you 2 to 1 – but for gawds sake don't broadcast it."

Two pound notes changed hands and Speedy took a long swig of pale ale to steady his nerves as he made a note in his book.

The Warrant Officers and Sergeants Mess annual shoot at the Seven Tunnel Range was in full swing. The bar was doing excellent business, the lunch tables groaned under the weight of cold cuisine and from the firing point the shots rang out, accompanied by only an occasional burst of curses or recrimination. The field telephone tinkled into life and Speedy took down the latest scores and updated the tote board. He felt a bead of sweat on his forehead; the favourite was starting to forge ahead and it was time to act. The message went down the line. "On the next shoot it's three eight and six two. You got that? 38 and 62 - good! We are moving to the four hundred yard mark in a few minutes."

As he finished speaking three cows sauntered across the front of the butts and the shooting stopped temporarily as the firing point officer raised his hat in solemn acknowledgement of the 'right to roam'. Just as well thought Speedy; last year someone had shot a prime bullock! Naturally the shot had been unintentional but nonetheless a 'bull' had been scored. The farmer had been understanding but he still demanded compensation.

Speedy checked the odds again and calculated the book. It was not looking good but he did not doubt the odds would swing in his favour at any moment and with only a moderate amount of assistance. He was just beginning to feel sanguine when he noted a mix-up. CSM Pugh, in shooting terms known to one and all as 'Blind Pugh', had moved to position six and Sergeant Riley had moved to position three. Oh shit, he thought as he called out. "Sar'nt Major! There's a cock up. Two firers have changed places."

The Sar'nt Major gave a cheery wave as he downed half a pint, "Piss off, Speedy! You run the Tote – I'll run the shoot."

As the firers settled and loaded, Speedy was rapidly reassessing the odds. He had just issued instructions that meant the person on firing point three got a minimum of eight bulls while firing point six would score very, very low. Bollocks, he thought, just as the odds were about to favour the poor bloody bookie! He looked heavenwards in search of rain but the sky was relentlessly blue, the cows refused to intervene and his frantic phone call went unanswered. The targets appeared, the future was in the lap of the gods; he crossed his fingers – 'how could you be so cruel?'

"Cheer up, Speedy; it's not the end of the world!" CSM Kidd tried to sound cheerful even though it was Monday morning. He looked carefully at Sergeant Swift and decided that the current rumours circulating that the poor soul may cut his own throat were at best premature. The man looked more shell shocked than suicidal.

Poor Speedy continued to look morose and there was a dullness in his eyes that was more than just sadness. He gave a deep sigh as he adjusted his typewriter; when he spoke it was with deep dejection.

"I lost twenty six quid! Twenty six bleedin' quid I tell you."

The CSM whistled in amazement, "Weeo! That's a lot!"

"You're telling me!"

"What went wrong – I thought you'd got it all organised."

"So did I. I got Bennet put in charge of the score cards in the butt party. Also it was agreed that after last year's cock-up the firing point places were to be nominated by a random draw at the start of the day so each person fired in turn according to the list and no coaching was to be allowed. That meant I knew exactly who was to shoot and when and alongside who. Naturally it was expected that Riley might win but just when I got the chance to nobble him, 'Blind Pugh' fucks it all up by moving position."

"How'd that happen?"

"He claimed the sun had been reflecting in his glasses."

"Didn't you protest?"

"Course I did. I tried to ring Bennet to change my instructions but no one answered the phone. So there we are – Blind Pugh is putting bullets into the Seven Tunnel and getting the flag meant for Riley, while Riley is getting a bull every bleedin' shot whether he hits the target or no! Riley got such a lead that no one could touch him. At least 'Blind Pugh' should have got a place with my help, but no, he never even scored another point. He'd had so much to drink he couldn't even walk to the bar upright."

"You should have lowered the odds."

"I did but it was too late. When I dropped the odds they all kept their hands in their pockets. Even the RSM copped me for a fiver and he was the blighter who let Pugh change! To add insult to injury Blind Pugh had backed himself for the lowest score – half a crown at twenty to one"

"There's always another time. I'll make sure I attend next year. That's the last baby we're going to have, I'll tell you!"

"How do you know that?"

"My Missis said 'conjugals' is out from now on. She ses her mother reckons it's disgusting having carnal knowledge at our age – bitch! – by the way, how did our butt party do?"

"At the end of the shoot they volunteered to help clear up. They ate every single morsel of food left over and drained

every glass – the plates were so clean they hardly needed washing! Would have been really good except for one thing."
"What was that?"
"They stopped the lorry on the way back and traded all the bloody empties and crates at the pub on Tutshill. Said they thought they weren't wanted. Now the Mess Treasurer wants thirty two shillings from me to square his accounts. When I get my hands on Bennet I'm going to castrate him!"
"D'you think it might have been Bennet who pissed in the C.O's karr-raff?"
"Only if he could have made money from it – and he certainly couldn't have filled if he'd been thinking of a young woman!"

The siren sounded and the approach to the 'Fire Station Shed' suddenly became a danger zone as eight apprentices, hyped up from several days of expectation, raced to do their duty. Already the Duty Fire Sergeant had turned over the engine of the fire truck and he switched on while lowering the window. He put his head out, "Get on! Move yourselves!"
A rap on the headboard told him the crew were aboard and he dipped the clutch, banged in the gear and accelerated away. He knew it was a practise run, the lads knew it was a practise run and the RSM who had lit the fire and set the alarm off knew that it was a practise run but God help anyone who didn't take it seriously.
The Bedford truck juddered to a halt. "Fire crew out!"
In a smooth display of careful and well rehearsed fire drill the team jumped into action, each setting about his allotted task. Two runs of hose sped out, the joint connected. As the pump engine fired into life the hose was connected in and the call went out. "Hose ready!"
"Declare water pressure!"
"Water pressure eighty!"

A Sin to Tell a Lie

The two lads gripping the nozzle end braced themselves, "Valve open – water on!"

The order was repeated, "Valve open – water on!" The hose surged and a jet of water sprayed out – straight up in the air as the hose bucked with the pressure.

The Fire Sergeant uttered a wild curse as he ran to the engine to lower the pressure. "What the fuck are you doing, Woolsey?"

"Valve is stuck, Sarge."

The nozzle twisted to the right as the pressure hit a 110 psi; the two hose men clung on but they managed to spray half the spectators before wrenching the head around. Unable to control the jet of water they watched in horrified fascination as the NAAFI manager's car filled with water through an open window.

At last the valve answered to the desperate measures applied to it and the pressure lowered; to almost everyone's disappointment. The fire was still alight.

The RSM put his pace stick under his left arm and stepped forward, a frozen grimace on his face, his voice grimmer. "What is wrong, Sergeant Hansen?"

"Valve stuck, Sar'nt Major."

"Have you fixed it?"

"Yessir."

"Back to your shed. We shall have another go."

"But what about the car, Sar'nt Major?"

The eyes narrowed. "If you spray it again I shall take it as deliberate disobedience to a direct order and you will kiss goodbye to your bleedin' pension. Now, before you go put up one of your 'Fire Drill' signs."

The fire alarm sounded for the second time as the NAAFI manager stepped out of the doorway and saw a reinvigorated bonfire flare up. Several hundred spectators fell silent and stared at him in expectation. It wasn't until he opened the door of his car that a glimmer of understanding descended on him! Several inches of water poured out soaking his shoes. It was as he started cursing out loud that the voice of reason penetrated his anger. The majestic body of the RSM towered over him. "Now, now, Mr Bright. We can't have swearing in front of the ladies – it's not nice – and rather un-gentlemanly."

Mr Bright was not mollified, his face red with anger. "Who is responsible for this outrage! Who is responsible – tell me that! One of your bloody lunatics I've no doubt!"

The dulcet tone continued. "If you will kindly move your car, Sir, I shall be obliged; this area is designated for fire drill as you can clearly see from the signs." The pacestick pointed. "It was very unwise to leave the window open."

"Move it! Fuckin' move it! It may never go again!"

"I shall get half a dozen boys to give you a push. They are trained mechanics as you no doubt know."

"Not bloody likely! If that lot get their hands on it I may never see it again."

The Fire Engine roared into view. "As you wish, Sir but there may be rather a lot of water in a moment." He smartly about turned and marched off, "Sergeant Hansen, control that valve!"

Bill Lucie cast emotional comments on my parental ancestry and bestowed a look of sheer dislike in my direction. It was only the fact that it was barely a minute past six a.m., half an hour before Reveille even, and my senses were numbed that prevented me from retaliating. Bill however held the high moral ground and he was annoyed, so he persevered "Why'd you call the CSM an arsehole?"

We were faced with a whole week of dining room duty. Up at six and on duty until eight pm; cleaning the company dining room and servery and serving out four meals each day to the whole company.

A Sin to Tell a Lie

"I didn't call him an arsehole. Besides which you laughed. Don't blame me for that! Come on!" We stepped into the cookhouse. Moments later we staggered back with a chest of bread and ten packets of margarine. Bill was still upset, "If anyone puts his plate too close I shall break it."

The cooked meals always arrived in large containers and plates were offered up for the food to be dished out. Hold the plate low and there was the good chance of heavy splatter or the food missing the plate altogether; hold the plate too high and the heavy metal spoon could shatter the plate as it dropped down. If the plate was held in the wrong position the server could vent his anger, annoyance, dislike etc by either ruining the food or smashing the plate! The Cook Sergeant peered out from the kitchen, "Get a move on you two!"

Containers of milk and cereal and trays of fried food appeared. The clock ticked by remorselessly; we weren't ready but the first wave of the ravening horde was already queuing at the door. The Orderly Sergeant arrived, concerned at the delay. "Let'em in – get a move on."

"We can't find the utensils!" He showed us where they were.

The doors opened and our first 'guests' arrived in a rush. Bill raised his outsize spoon in an intimidating gesture, his face angry, "Stop pushing or you'll get buggerall!" There was instant order.

The person serving was in a powerful position; he could, within certain bounds, dispense in a miserly way or distribute largesse. At that moment as he served he held more power over hungry lads than the Commandant.

Forty minutes later the company had gone and we sat eating our breakfast. We were both surprised at how little waste there was – and almost nothing spilt! The duty cook had done us a very nice fresh eggs and bacon and there was a plentiful supply of everything to eat including a bit of properly fried bread, a

A Sin to Tell a Lie

rare treat. Bill wiped the egg yolk off his plate and savoured the taste. "I think I'll do a bit of toast and I might manage some marmalade."

I passed him a packet of best butter, "Try that – it tastes better."

"Where'd that come from?"

"Just be nice to the cook – we can have what we want to eat."

Bill looked around us and the cleaning that had to be done, "If we get stuck in we can be finished in an hour - then we can put our feet up until dinnertime. That's the best breakfast I've had since Christmas."

It was obvious we could eat like fighting cocks. "Steady Bill, we're safe here. No parades, no barrack room duties and if we play our cards right there are a few nice little earners. Will Castell reckons we should make a couple of quid easy."

Bill looked a bit dubious, "I dunno. Sounds a bit dangerous to me."

"Bollocks! I want Saturday off so I need to make some dosh to pay someone to stand in for me. Besides which we just pass everything straight to Will and share the proceeds with him – dead easy."

Bill still looked dubious, "That's robbin' our mates."

"OK then, if you want to be Robin bleedin' Hood we'll give it all to our mates."

Bill nodded agreement, "Don't worry about Saturday; Ted will do dinner and tea just to get extra rations."

"Right, let's have another cuppa tea – then we'll start. By the way, I'll do the wash tank - OK" The wash tank was two feet deep and filled with hot soapy water so the lads could clean their plates as they left. I'd got three tins of strawberry jam and two tins of baked beans residing there awaiting collection! This week was to be used to my advantage as soon as I learnt to mark the tins before the labels fell off!

A Sin to Tell a Lie

JULY 1952

For me the summer and cricket could never arrive quickly enough and the arrival of July would have been sad except that the rehearsals for the passing out parade heralded the quickening approach of summer leave; but the early days were dominated by the School Gymkhana and the Drumhead Service. This was when the apprentices and staff combined to try and relieve any passer-by of their cash to support the local charity i.e. the aforementioned apprentices and staff and their families. As usual the sun shone on the ungodly and the serious business of collecting the equivalent of 'Dane geld' began. By devious means, mainly via an army strategy known as 'never volunteer', I had managed to evade the duty list and soon I was walking hand in hand with my newly found Susan among the stalls. We were generally of a like mind on most things but in the excitement and carnival atmosphere she lost her sense of caution and actually started to believe the siren calls to 'roll up! roll up! win your fortune here' and sundry other enticements. With squeals of delight and open handbag she skittered from stall to stall losing first her own money and then, when that was gone, demanding mine. When I started to refuse the smile slipped, the lips became petulant and the summer day started to grow decidedly cooler.

"It's only sixpence for a ticket!"
"I never took you for a meanie!"
"I thought we came here to enjoy ourselves!"
"If you're going to be mean I'm going home!"
"Brian Woolsey wouldn't treat me like this – he knows how to treat a girl."
"That's it – I'm going home, so there!"
"I never want to see you again!"

Twenty minutes after the first complaint she was off. Momentarily at a loss as to how to deal with my new found freedom I stood watching Sergeant Swift operate the wheel of fortune. It took me a while to work out what was happening. He kept up a constant patter while judging the betting pattern on the marked table where all the numbers on the wheel were replicated in a square. As soon as a decent amount of money had been laid down he would set the wheel spinning and clicking. It was obvious that if the wheel was left to its own devices some bias favoured three adjacent particular numbers to win; these were allowed to win if the betting was small but as soon as the repeated pattern drew in the larger bets he would set the wheel spinning and a random number would click in! My admiration for a professional increased. To control the wheel he was obviously modifying a weight where his hand held the wheel at about the 'ten o'clock' position, because it was that number that always finished at or close to 'six o'clock' when it suited. The new winning number being at twelve o'clock.

I had half a crown when I set down my first bet. Within half an hour I had twelve shillings.

Sergeant Swift jerked his head, "Come here, Elks."

"Yes, Sarge?"

He moved two steps sideways, "Did you know I'm a watchful old cove?"

I couldn't think of an answer so I tried to look humble as he continued "Yes, in my time Elks, I've been fucked about by experts – so I know when I'm being fucked about." He fixed me with gimlet eyes, his glasses magnified the effect so I was transfixed, "You're a lucky little sod!" In another life he would have made an expert ventriloquist because his lips hardly moved.

A Sin to Tell a Lie

"Dunno about that, Sarge," I tried to look miserable, pathetic, sad and hurt all at the same time, "I lost my girl this afternoon."

"Well, your name is in my book and if you don't piss off your luck will get even worse!"

As I went to catch the bus later in the day, eager to exploit my new found freedom among the young ladies of Chepstow I was whistling a tune, as usual ---

'On top of Old Smokey, all covered with snow
I lost my true lover for courting too slow
For courting's a pleasure but partings are grief
And a false hearted lover is worse than a thief
A thief will just rob you and take what you have
But a false hearted lover will lead you to the grave……..'

Once again that perfect peace that signalled the departure of the last bus carrying apprentices to the railway station heralded the beginning of the summer leave period. Ronnie Marsden relished these few weeks of sublime peace and sunshine with a degree of appreciation with which he had once viewed the female form undressed; that of course was a long time ago before he started to suffer from 'erectile impairment' as the doctor so kindly put it. In the Tank Corp this affliction had been known as 'weapon fatigue' but in those good old days it had often been boosted about, as it was claimed it was caused by overuse! Now he knew differently as the stresses and heavy strains of military leadership and administration at Beachley took their toll. His office door was open and he could hear Sergeant Swift humming as he made a pot of tea.

A Sin to Tell a Lie

CSM Kidd stepped in the doorway, "Good morning, Sir. The lads have all gone, bless'em. I just thought I would let you know I've inspected the barrack rooms and all is well - no nasty paintwork today, ha ha!"

Ronnie wiped the smile from his face as he scowled, "Just as well Sar'nt Major – otherwise we would be raffling one of your bollocks!"

The Colonel had suggested that the RSM stand at ease but it was clear from his posture that this particular military drill position had been deleted from the manual of instruction issued to, and always followed without question, by Grenadier Guardsmen in the presence of God or his second in command. He remained alert but as rigid as the ram-rod that was obviously stuck up his backside. Actually he wanted a pee but when the Colonel called he must obey immediately; the only indication of the bodily demand was a slight induration and perflation of the lower abdominal musculature adjacent to his testicles and a very small nervous tic in his left eyeball. "You called, Sir!" His right foot perforated the carpet.

"Very sorry to trouble you at this moment, Sergeant Major but this must be dealt with now. Have you by any chance lost a pair of pyjamas of late?"

"As a matter of fact I have, Sir. Two weeks ago my wife said that a pair of my pyjamas had gone missing, perhaps stolen, from her washing line. She had left them out overnight."

"I believe they may have been found."

"Thank you, Sir. They are a rather expensive item to replace."

"Your thanks may be premature. I have just received a complaint from the Chepstow Town Council Clerk that they appear to be flying from the flagpole on the wall of Chepstow Castle."

The left eyelid moved involuntarily for the first time in seventeen years of dedicated service. "Surely not, Sir."

A Sin to Tell a Lie

"The Clerk cannot be sure, naturally, because they can only be viewed through binoculars. But he claims they contain a message and your name. They are trying to get them down but the halliards are twisted. They are worried that the flagpole may break in this wind."

"Do you wish me to take any action in this matter, Sir?"

"Not directly. I believe that C Company may be implicated so I am going to send Captain Marsden and the Adjutant to deal with this. Dear me, you really don't look well, Sergeant Major; I suggest you take the rest of the day off. Perhaps Mrs Baker will make you a nice cup of tea."

Flying High!

The Castle Warden bristled as the two officers approached, though as a public employee he maintained a semblance of good manners. Nonetheless he could not keep the irritation from his voice. "I've been waiting over an hour. The reporter from the South Wales Gazette was here an hour since!"

The Adjutant poured oil onto troubled waters, "We came as soon as we heard, Mr Bates. I apologise for this misdemeanour. We shall use our best endeavours to track down the culprit. Always supposing it is our men at fault, that is."

That earned a reproachful look and a loud sniff, "Bound to be your lot. What I can't understand is how they did it."

"Perhaps you could explain please." Ronnie tried to sound polite.

"Well it's like this. That airship up there," he pointed, "wasn't hoisted last night when I locked up. I locked the inner gate and the outer gate having made sure everyone had left – besides which there were no visitors after three o'clock. Our home is over there so I can keep an eye on things. We never left the house and I unlocked the outer gate this morning at nine thirty when I got the telephone call from the Town Clerk."

"When will you have this object down?"

"Come with me – two council workmen are doing it at this moment. I tell you though, I've never seen pyjamas that big in all my life."

"How do you think the intruders got in?"

"It's a complete mystery, there are great big walls all around; the gates are solid. It must have been done by parachute."

Ronnie swallowed a couple of 'Rennies' as his stomach griped. "May we see the flag site, Mr Bates?"

"This way."

They inspected the evidence while the Council workmen struggled to repair the halliards. The Adjutant stroked his chin whilst giving the pyjamas a thorough inspection. Someone had sewn the jacket to the trousers so it would fly like an airship. Daubed across it were the words, 'BUSTY BAKERs BLOOMERS', in grey paint. Underneath was a large 'C'

A Sin to Tell a Lie

followed by a squiggle. Ronnie breathed a sigh of relief. "I don't think that means it was done by C Company."

The Adjutant nodded, "No, but that's definitely a pair of army pyjamas – a very large pair – small wonder the halliards broke under the strain!"

Mr Bates frowned and his eyes blinked. "I hope you're not trying to evade responsibility, gentlemen."

The Adjutant was emphatic in reply. "No, we will foot the bill for the repair of the halliards – the Commandant would be most concerned otherwise. What I fail to understand is how the culprits got in if you locked up properly."

"I know my duty. I've been doing it for twenty years!"

"Perhaps we may inspect the grounds, with your permission of course."

Speedy looked up from his typewriter. "I've never known our Captain to disappear so fast in all my time here."

CSM Kidd nodded agreement, "You're right. Mind you, he was a worried man when the message came this morning and he thought it had been done by C Company. D'you know, he was actually smiling when he left just now. Perhaps that's just what he needs to overcome the 'Brewer's Droop' his wife is complaining about."

"He still checked his office and carafe to make sure they hadn't been tampered with – do you think he'll ever forgive the little blighter that did that?"

"Where are you going on holiday, Speedy?"

"I'll tell you where I'm not going – I'm not going rock climbing?"

"D'you reckon that's how they got into the castle?" CSM Kidd's forehead knotted up in concentration as he thought about it, just as it did when he was sitting maths in the Second Class Examinations.

A Sin to Tell a Lie

"Well. They didn't use a parachute, did they!"

"The RSM and the Provo Sergeant are compiling lists from the 'Booking Out Book' of all the lads leaving camp yesterday evening – but that's a waste of blooming time. Whoever did it won't be that daft!"

Speedy smiled. "I reckon we ought to promote whoever did it. Should be made a colonel, at least." He typed in the last word on the return, released the paper and removed the carbons. "Definitely officer material in my view."

"The Q.M. has said he's indented for another pair of pyjamas for the RSM but for the moment he'll have to sleep every other week in the nuddy. Apparently another factory has got to be opened so there will be a short delay. The whole economy of the Lancashire cotton mills has been revived."

Speedy removed the report with a touch of triumphalism. "There – all done! Let's have a cuppa tea and call it a day. I reckon we deserve a break for a few weeks."

"The company dance is all organised for the end of September. I hope you've got some new tunes for us."

"Don't you fret, Harry. By the way, have you heard the one about the apprentice's medical parade?"

"Can't say I have."

"There was this army apprentice school just back from summer leave and a company commander parades his lot before the M.O. for inspection. Him and the Medico are walking together, side by side, along the rows of lads who are all lined up with their trousers down and their equipment on display when they come to this lad standing there with a bloody great erection sticking out. The Commander is affronted and he pokes the lad in the chest with his stick. "Disgraceful! Get rid of that immediately!" he demanded.

"I can't, Sir," replied the lad, "It's because we've been on leave for four weeks."

A Sin to Tell a Lie

The officer was so mad he gave the erection a real whack with his stick. "That'll teach you, you little sod!" he roared.

The M.O. stepped forward, concern on his face. "No more of that please. Did that hurt, soldier?"

"No, Sir - but I believe Apprentice Smith behind me wishes to make a formal complaint regarding the cruel assault of a deadly weapon."

CSM Kidd scratched his head and looked puzzled. "What was the lad Smith complaining about?"

Speedy reached for the teapot; Bollocks! he thought.

"Ho, I get it, Speedy – but I've never heard of an officer's stick being called a deadly weapon!"

"'Ear – drink this before ……, forget it!"

A Sin to Tell a Lie
THE ROBOT
The following was extracted from the December 1952 copy and relates to the period **Feb 1952 to Sept 1952**.

PRIZE WINNERS 50B

Vehicle Mechanics	A Bassett, F Cresswell, H Kemp
Electricians	H Finnamore, G Stone
Fitters	R Wooton, R Sirett
Sheet Metal Workers	M Spinks
Education	H Finnamore, M Medhurst, D Whatley

REPRESENTATIVE COLOURS 50A & 50B

Full	A Burden, R Commins, D Leswell, J Overend (Athletics) M Buckland, B Elks, R Wooton, R Hewton.(Cricket)
Half	P Baugh, B Ennew, J Harrington, H Maisey, B Woolsey (Athletics)

WELSH NATIONAL AAA YOUTHS   W Dallas, 1st long jump.

FORCES PRELIM EXAM (50A & 50B)   P Baugh, W Castell, H Finnamore, R Rowell.

FIRST CLASS CERTIFICATE OF EDUCATION (50A & 50B)
F Cresswell, A Bassett, R Barnett, T Denton, L Drury, B Elks, H Finnamore, R Foster, J Kinson, M Kimber, A Levitt, D Lewin, M Medhurst, J Porter, B Rowson, T Sandford, D Talling, D Whatley, H Williams.

NUMBERS OF QUALIFIED TRADESMEN PASSING OUT, 49B

Vehicle Mechanics	49
Electricians	7
Control Equipment Electricians	7
Fitters	23
Blacksmiths	2
Sheet Metal Workers	9
Total	97

October 1952

Our winter evenings were often enlivened by compulsory attendance at boxing matches. Very few lads were actually interested in boxing and most would rather have gone into town to wrestle with young ladies. However the army considered that non participation in boxing must mean that you were suffering from an abject and demeaning form of self denial of pain. In their desire to provoke and stimulate our martial spirits and stifle the pangs of denial, we were required to attend as many boxing matches as possible and watch one lad try to knock the shit out of another. The actual ejection was infrequent but none the less a brush and pan was always close by the judges in case the ring needed cleaning between bouts. If the athletics field could be described as the home of 'Olympian Endeavour' then the Gymnasium on boxing night was most certainly the Roman Coliseum, populated by martial gladiators and bloodthirsty spectators.

.

The season started with the school championships and inter-company wars followed by set piece battles against other army and RAF establishments. Some Boxing Establishments were so taken with our facilities and myriad noisy support that they came from far and wide to pay penance and display their fighting skills at this temple of pugilism. There was however a facet of spectator participation that confounded me. While the two boxers in the ring were trying to punch out the lights of their opponent the spectators must remain in total silence. Not a pin must drop! Not even a sniff or, god forbid, a fart! As soon as the bell rang to start a bout you made any sound or noise at your peril. One boxer described the silence as terrifying; that was when the pain started. The only noise was the smack of leather on skin and the occasional command of the referee. The next bell was obliterated by an explosion of

A Sin to Tell a Lie

shouting and calling while the seconds worked their magic with sponges, water and towel; followed by a welter of instructions most of which were lost in the cacophony of noise. All designed to stimulate the flow of adrenalin, wash away the pain and propel the unwilling back into conflict once more.
'Don't worry lad, these new plastic surgeons can do wonders.'
'He's tiring!'
'– of course he's tiring', he's wore hisself out because he keeps on bleedin' hitting me!

The story of the man too proud to run

'HIGH NOON'

STANLEY KRAMER PRODUCTIONS
GARY COOPER
HIGH NOON

A Sin to Tell a Lie

On most boxing nights my partisanship was somewhat whimsical but tonight that was a mate in the ring and he was fighting desperately but rather foolishly against a better boxer; too damn proud to call it a night by falling over but strong enough to remain upright, despite the punishment. So the fight went the full three rounds and I winced with each blow until at last the MC raised the glove of the inevitable winner.

It was nearly nine thirty as we walked back to the barrack room. "I think you ought to give it up, Brian."

His face was puffing up nicely so his voice was temporarily slurred. "Ishno rite thash whar."

I hoped his brain wasn't in the same state. "Don't worry; we won't be here next winter. Some other twerp can get knocked about." I scrutinised his face, "You won't be going to the dance on Saturday at this rate."

I stood beside him in the washroom as he held his face under a basin of cold water. He came up for air surprisingly articulate, "Miss the dance! Not bloody likely – you'll pinch my girl." His face went under again and I wrung out the towel.

"I'm not after your girl!" Who the hell would want a girl who too obviously favoured a prize fighter's broken nose and black eyes. I handed over the towel again and inspected his facial bruises, "But I'll tell you what. You won't be able to eat tomorrow – I'll have your dinner - OK?"

"You pay for my dance ticket this weekend, it's a deal." There was a dance at the 'Hut' at Bulwark on Saturday evening.

I lit a symbol of suave masculine sex appeal and success, a Woodbine cigarette, and offered him a puff. "Agreed."

He wound the cool wet towel around his face. "What d'you think of the new march, 'The Army Apprentice'?"

"Alright I suppose – not much of a tune is it?"

"It'll never catch on like 'High Noon'."

"You hum it - I'll sing it."

'Do not forsake me, oh my darling,
  On this our wedding day.
Do not forsake me oh my darling,
  Wait-----wait alone.
I do not know what fate awaits me,
  I only know I must be brave
For I must face the man who hates me,
  Or lie a coward, a craven coward
  Or lie a coward in my grave ....'

November 1952

"Will you listen to me! What are you going to do about it?" The NAAFI manageress may have been naked and vulnerable to attack from both frontal and rear assault but she was certainly not defenceless while her tongue roamed free. Henry Winter, Provost Sergeant and cruel enforcer of regulations and sadistic pleasure taker of lads on jankers, answered meekly.
"I don't know, Iris. Are you sure there's a problem?" He sounded a mite distracted but then he really had his mind on other things nearer to his brains.
"Stop poking that flamin' weapon at me and listen!"
"Yes, Love. Whatever you say, my Love."
"Don't you try and soft soap me, Henry Winters – I expect action!"
Henry sniffed as he thought, that's what I'm trying to do. Women could be so cruel on occasion. "Tell me again, Love."
Her voice got sharper, "As I said, food is going missing from the Cold Store. I checked yesterday at six before we opened the NAAFI, then again this morning. I wrote down what's missing."

'B' COMPANY RUGBY TEAM 52/53

Henry read the list impatiently. "There's not a lot gone. Perhaps it's mice."

Iris was unimpressed. "Don't talk daft! It's a cold store, specially protected and locked. Besides which, if it was mice, there would be some sign of them." She reached for the list. "Listen to this. Eight portions of fruit cake, four iced slices, four bananas and four meat pasties. Does that sound like mice to you?"

"Did your staff go in there after you checked?"

"No - and the key never left my person."

"Where do you keep the key?"

"Not where you've got your flaming hand! Give over."

"Sorry my Love, I was thinking."

"Well, stop thinking with your dick! The store is only forty yards from the Guardroom and you pass it every time you creep in here – surely you must notice something going on."

The RSM seemed very calm and collected but it was obvious he was mildly annoyed. He didn't like being beaten so he spoke rather tersely. "Report, Sergeant Winter."

"Unfortunately the manageress's reports are confirmed. Over the last two weeks food has disappeared from the cold store on two occasions. Only smallish amounts – but definitely theft; it's always easily consumed fruit and foodstuffs such as cake. According to the manageress this had occurred at least five times prior to this – and perhaps before that, before she noticed. Always, so it seems, between six in the evening and nine a.m."

"Apprentices?"

"I believe so from what is taken."

"How do they get in?"

"That is a mystery. There are two sets of keys. One set is kept securely locked in the Guardroom. During workshop hours only the civilian instructor is allowed to book them out, otherwise they are only issued to the duty officer if there is a problem. The manageress has the other set."

"Which is the civilian instructor?"

"Mr Jones. He's been maintaining the refrigeration plant for years and uses it to teach apprentices about refrigeration operation and maintenance."

"That's it then. I bet the little buggers have copied the keys!"

Sergeant Winter suppressed a smile. "My first thought, Sar'nt Major but Mr Jones only takes out the refrigeration room key. He leaves the cold room key in the guardroom. The cold room has a separate locked door. Cold salt water is pumped via pipes from the refrigerator into the cold room."

"My, my, you have been thorough, Sergeant. It sounds to me as if you've been in hot water with all these complaints from the manageress." His eyebrows rose.

"I do my best to maintain good relations with the civilian staff, Sar'nt Major."

"So I've heard. You should be careful; she has a reputation for tying men to her bed with handcuffs if given the chance. We wouldn't want you locked up now, would we?"

Sergeant Winters felt it was best to ignore such innuendo. "As I was saying, Sar'nt Major. Mr Jones has sworn he has not booked out the cold room key since last Christmas. If there is equipment failure an alarm rings. If Mr Jones is not on duty we call out the apprentice fitters nominated by Mr Jones but the apprentices are not permitted to have the keys. The duty officer draws the keys and unlocks – he closely supervises the apprentices at all times and locks up when the plant is working. As you are aware, the duty officer changes every day."

"Who are these apprentices?"

"Around half a dozen sixth term lads – all with unblemished records. Quite a few are NCO's. I don't believe it's them."

Oh you asshole, thought the RSM, of course it's them; or if not them, then their mates. "We must put a stop to this,

Sergeant. Have your patrols check both doors every hour from lights out to reveille – and perhaps you wouldn't mind checking yourself, as you pop round to see the manageress. Naturally we must try to maintain friendly relations—mustn't we?"

"I try to keep her happy, Sar'nt Major."

The nose wrinkled and sniffed, "Perhaps if she were to moderate her shouts of happiness as you bring her to the boil you may hear the intruders getting into the cold store."

December 1952

The torchlight held me firmly in its grip; it was a fair cop. I tried to stop my eyes blinking in the unexpected beam because that seemed to convey guilt. It did no good as I was obviously a master criminal caught 'in the act'. Lance Corporal Gilbert, camp provost staff, had got me; I could detect the triumph in his voice. "Stand still, soldier!" The torchlight mover closer to my nose, "Got you, you thieving sod! Stand to attention in the presence of an NCO."

I put my feet together in the correct posture of servitude but I wasn't worried. Corporal Gilbert wasn't as bright as his torch but he would understand he had made a mistake as soon as I explained.

Corporal Gilbert was entirely suited to his role because both he and his role were so easily disliked, especially by apprentices. The unfortunate Gilbert had a face that even a mother might baulk at and his left eye had a habit of entering a wandering orbit. It is very difficult to look at two eyes at once especially when the owner was liable to mistake your attempt as insubordination and thereby provoke retribution. He also wore two 'Good Conduct' stripes but we were convinced his good behaviour arose not from a desire to be good but from insufficient intelligence to get into trouble.

UNIT HOCKEY XI, 1952-1953

Winners, Mid-West District Championship; Western Command Championship; U.K. Championship; runners-up Army Inter-Unit Championship.

A Sin to Tell a Lie

"I'm taking this tray to our party, Corp." I proffered up the tray for inspection.

"How did you get in the cold store?" He checked the door but found it was locked

"I haven't been in the cold store."

"There's been thieving here for months, so don't lie to me! Where's the key? " He checked me over.

"I haven't got any keys!" I answered rather sharply, "And this has been paid for – we're having a party in our barrack room."

"Don't get cheeky with me or you'll be in even worse fuckin' trouble!" The torch lowered and he searched the ground. "The key is here."

"We paid for this."

The torch searched my face again. Lance Corporal Gilbert obviously looked upon it as the means of illuminating the truth, "I don't believe you. Where's your proof?"

"We paid the NAAFI manageress over an hour ago. Ask her."

"Ah! Gotcha! Don't try to fool me, soldier. The manageress went out with Sergeant Winter as soon as the NAAFI closed for the evening – at least thirty minutes ago. I know because she spoke to me – and she never mentioned you lot picking up cakes from the cold store." His voice became triumphant.

I tried patient argument but the contempt asserted itself, "We bought three trays, not one- not two – but three! – and this is the last one. Only the manageress went in the bloody store! We left this tray until last so it would stay cool."

"If you paid for it, where's the receipt?" Sherlock Holmes couldn't have put it better!

"She didn't give us one."

"Right, you're under close arrest for theft! I've had enough of your lying bollocks and cheek!"

"My mates are waiting to eat these cakes."

"Those cakes are evidence! To the guardroom, quick march! Left, right, left! There's a nice cell waiting for you, soldier."

SCHOOL RUGBY TEAM 52/53

A Sin to Tell a Lie

Sergeant Winter looked at me, then he looked at Corporal Gilbert, then he shook his head several times as if he was exasperated with both of us. The clock said it was one a.m. Three hours in an uncomfortable cell had seemed an eternity; made worse by the fact that although I knew I was innocent I had no faith in the provost hierarchy's ability to accept that fact. However the cell was unlocked and I was beckoned out. Sergeant Winter glared at me. "Stand to attention!" He turned to Corporal Gilbert, "I've checked with the manageress and she confirms this soldier's story."

Lance Corporal Gilbert looked glum; his triumph in solving the cold store crime of the century was in ruins. Only a few minutes ago I had overheard the two talking and the Provost Sergeant using the words 'arsehole' rather frequently.

The Corporal defended himself. "The circumstances were very suspicious, Sergeant and he was extremely insolent when questioned."

"D'you hear that, soldier? You come the old soldier again and I shall charge you myself. I can't stand a smartarse – d'you understand me?"

I thought a protest may rebound on me so I was duly humble, "Yes, Sarge."

"Take those cakes and get to bed. If you're not in bed asleep in five minutes you'll be charged with disobeying a direct order. Move yourself!"

The call came the next morning, I was to report to the company office immediately. CSM Kidd greeted my arrival with a solemn stare and just a hint of satisfaction, his index finger beckoned me in. "It seems our paths are destined to cross rather frequently, Elks." He licked his lips and rubbed his hands together as if in anticipation of some coming pleasure.

A Sin to Tell a Lie

I crossed my fingers and hoped that his words weren't true; I couldn't think of a reply that may not be misinterpreted so I kept quiet.

His eyes studied a list. "You were absent from roll call last night according to the orderly sergeant." His eyebrows raised, "No doubt you can relate a funny story or excuse for my amusement regarding this absence." It was obvious I had not been forgiven for the asteroids.

"I was under close arrest in the guardroom at roll call, Sar'nt Major."

The broadest of broad beamed smiles slowly flooded his face and his shoulders trembled with suppressed mirth. I had no idea that beneath that stern exterior lived a man with a wicked sense of humour when the laugh was on me. "In a cell, you claim. Why aren't you still there?" The smile did not abate.

"It was a mistake, Sar'nt Major. Lance Corporal Gilbert thought I had stolen food from the cold store but I hadn't."

I had somehow expected sympathy but none was forthcoming because the broad smile remained intact.

"You were arrested? That's the kind of story I like, Elks. Who let you out?"

"Sergeant Winter."

"And what did Sergeant Winter say?"

"He said it was my fault for being a smartarse – even though I had done nothing wrong."

His prolonged and mocking laugh remained with me all the way back to the Workshop; as I marched down the hill I had time to ruminate on the cruelties of life. Another soldier's commandment commended itself to me; to be adopted as part of my armoury against the slings and arrows of outrageous fortune – 'thou shalt not piss-off your superior if he is in a position to retaliate'.

A Sin to Tell a Lie
THE ROBOT
The following was extracted from the June 1953 copy and relates to the period Sept **1952 to Feb 1953**.

PRIZE WINNERS 50A

Vehicle Mechanics	P Phillips, P Mason, I Rumble
Electricians	J Harris, D Leach
Fitters	T Gleeson, A Weyman
Sheet Metal Workers	A Morris
Blacksmiths	B Taylor
Education	P Baugh, R Taylor, D Leach
Sport	P Anzalucca, **Cyril Gallie Boxing Cup**
	P Mason, **Individual Athletics Cup.**

REPRESENTATIVE COLOURS 50A & 50B

Full	D Birchall, B Masters, W Dallas, R Clough, J Harrington, P Mason, R Bindloss (Football) B Rowson, H Maisey (Rugby) P Anzalucca, B Ennew, R Poingdestre, C Kennedy, A Milburn J Hogg, T Gleeson, J Castell (Boxing) R Wright, M Kimber R Barnett, R Wells (Shooting)
Half	M Tostevin, D Epps, J Wildish, E Woods (Football)

FORCES PRELIM EXAM (50A & 50B) R Scott, R Taylor

FIRST CLASS CERTIFICATE OF EDUCATION (50a & 50B)
M Allen, K Andrews, A Appleton, P Baugh, M Beresford, B Bull, J Bacon, P Brown, G Burgess, V Church, J Castell, W Dallas, K Down, B Ennew, T Fox, A George, J Gardner, M Gwinnell, R Harder, J Harrington, D Jacobs, R Jones, J Jowett, R Kemp, D Lee, A Morris, C Montague, K Nichols, G Pendle, F Puddy, C Robinson, R Rowell, R Sandall, A Skinner, J Selway, P Sturgess, R Scott, G Stone, R Wells, C Williams, R Wright, P Wallis, J Wildish, R Wort,

NUMBERS OF QUALIFIED TRADESMEN PASSING OUT, 50A

Vehicle Mechanics	47	Electricians	9
Control Equipment Electricians	8	Fitters	20
Blacksmiths	6	Sheet Metal Workers	12
	Total 102		

A Sin to Tell a Lie
THE 50A PASSING OUT LIST

TRADESMEN

The undermentioned Apprentices passed the Trade Test shown on the date stated:

Vehicle Mechanic, Group " A," Class III
12th December, 1952

22308164 M. B. Allen
22309171 A. E. Appleton
22289265 C. A. Ball
22309133 H. Barker
22309205 D. W. Boycott
22309141 J. B. Brennan
22289231 O. A. Cheek
22309186 J. Chew
22309162 J. H. Cox
22289226 W. E. Davies
22309165 W. A. Dewar
22289224 J. A. Farrant
22289209 K. F. Frampton
22309132 J. R. Hardy
22309159 P. R. Herrett
22289203 B. A. Homer
22309126 T. D. Ingles
22309125 D. A. Jacobs
22289278 B. O. Ketley
22289190 P. J. Mason
22289189 B. L. Masters
22309210 M. J. Matthews
22289244 R. McGreedy
22309177 A. Millburn
22289172 M. Millard
22309191 A. W. Milton
22309137 J. A. Neilson
22309163 G. P. Pendle
22309167 P. D. Phillips
22309121 A. R. Pitt-Pladdy
22309214 L. M. Porter
22309168 T. L. Price
22309131 A. B. Rhodes
22309189 I. R. Rumble
22289155 J. T. Sanders
22309123 A. E. Skinner
22309138 R. A. Smith
22289261 A. J. Stanger
22309201 C. Squire
22309187 K. Trowsdale
22309197 A. Turner
22309174 K. Walton
22309150 R. E. Wells
22309184 C. W. Williams
22309156 H. E. Williams
22309217 C. Winter
22289217 E. J. York

Electrician (Vehicle and Plant), Group " A," Class III
13th December, 1952

22309160 R. K. Barnett
22309116 M. A. Beresford
22289165 E. F. Charlton
22309222 V. G. Church
22309166 T. J. Denton
22274103 T. A. Hodgkinson
22289179 A. E. Howard
22309113 D. J. Leach
22309145 J. H. Moore

Electrician (Control Equipment) (A.A. and C.A.)
Group " A," Class III, 13th December, 1952

22309119 P. M. Baugh
22309122 L. Drury
22309128 R. H. Foster
22309130 J. H. Harris
22309152 B. Rowson
22309117 R. S. Sandall
22309115 R. Taylor
22289152 P. Webb

Fitter REME, Group " A," Class III
12th December, 1952

22309208 D. Bevan
22309190 A. D. Burdon
22309147 F. G. Dale
22309218 F. G. Davidson
22309120 F. C. English
22309223 M. J. Kimber
22309221 J. A. Kinson
22309142 A. F. Weyman

Fitter RE, Group " A," Class III, 12th December, 1952

22309192 R. T. Bindloss
22309213 R. Commins
22309154 B. Elliott
22309158 R. C. Hyde

Engine Fitter (I.C. and Pumps), Group " A," Class III,
12th December, 1952

22309196 P. A. Bignall
22309153 B. E. Bull
22309181 R. Day
22289233 E. Forster
22309143 T. M. Gleeson
22309200 F. S. Goddard
22309148 W. A. Graves
22309182 D. R. Leswell

Blacksmith, Group " B", Class III, 12th December, 1952

22309151 B. Banyard
22309202 R. S. Fahey
22309175 A. Fowler
22309155 R. J. Overd
22309212 R. K. Taylor
22309194 A. G. Vosper

Sheet Metal Worker, Group " B," Class III,
12th December, 1952

22309176 J. T. Bright
22309172 F. Butler
22309178 J. C. Marshall
22309149 A. Morris
22309146 A. J. Overd
22309193 G. G. Robinson
22309219 A. Theobald
22274117 K. Williams
22309335 N. A. Winter
22309211 D. Wood
22309220 E. J. Wood
22305533 R. J. Wright

A Sin to Tell a Lie

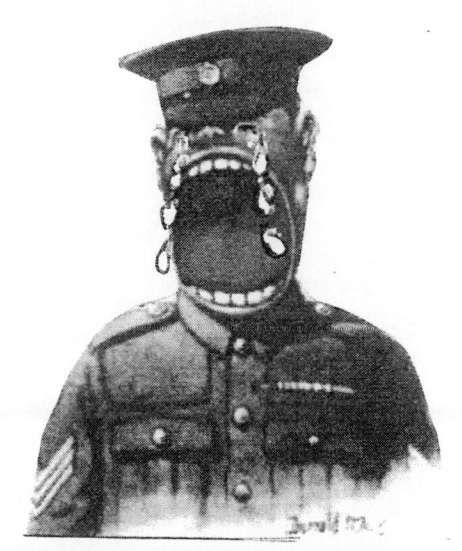

'GOODBYE LADS, I SHALL MISS YOU ALL!' SNIFF-SNIFF. 'ALL TOGETHER NOW 'WE'LL MEET AGAIN, DON'T KNOW................'

PASSING OUT PARADE 50A GROUP

February 1953

We had met before but she had been with someone else; she was quite beautiful. Our eyes had met briefly but I knew at that moment we would meet again. It was several weeks later when I nearly bumped into her as we passed in the narrow passageway under the town medieval gateway. We both stopped but now she was alone, we could speak but somehow it wasn't easy.

I stuttered a little in the confusion, "I - I'm - sorry..."

She went to walk on, "It was my fault - not looking..." She stopped.

I found my voice, "Are you alone?" She nodded. "Before – you know - I wanted to ask you out but....." My nerve gave out and my tongue went dry.

She said it shyly with just the hint of a smile, "You should have done – shall we have a coffee?"

My hope soared, "We could go to the pictures, perhaps..."

"Afterwards... I would like that."

I offered her my hand and she took it.

A Sin to Tell a Lie

Sam walks over to the piano and sees Ilsa sitting at the table.
Ilsa.   Hello Sam.
Sam.   Hello Miss Ilsa, I never expected to see you again.
Ilsa.   It's been a long time.
Sam.   Yes Mam, a lotta water under the bridge. (Sam sits down at the piano)
Ilsa.   Some of the old songs, Sam.
Sam.   Yes Mam. (He plays 'Avignon')
Ilsa   Where is Rick?
Sam.   I don't know – I aint seen him all night.
Ilsa.   When will he be back?
Sam.   Not tonight-no more-he aint coming-went home early.
Ilsa.   Does he always leave so early?
Sam.   Oh, he never – he's gotta girl – up at the Blue Parrot. He goes up there all the time.
Ilsa.   You used to be a much better liar, Sam.
Sam.   Leave him alone, Miss Ilsa. You bad luck for him.
Ilsa.   (smiles gently) Play it once, Sam - for old time's sake.

A Sin to Tell a Lie

Sam. *I don't know what you mean, Miss Ilsa.*
Ilsa. *Play it, Sam. Play 'As Time Goes By'.*
Sam. *I can't remember that, Miss Ilsa – I'm a little rusty on it.*
Ilsa. *I'll hum it for you - Di-Di Dee Di Dee Dum, Di-Di-Dee*
      - sing it, Sam.

In the darkness I slipped my arm around her shoulder and held her hand that seemed so cool. She moved closer and put her head on my shoulder. The smell of her hair with its faint touch of perfume pervaded my senses - such bliss. She squeezed my hand as Sam sang for us and Ingrid Bergman and I kissed her for the first time -

'You must remember this, a kiss is still a kiss
a sigh is just a sigh, the fundamental things apply
as time goes by.
And when two lovers woo they still say I love you
On that you can rely, no matter what the future brings
as time goes by.
Moonlight and love songs never out of date
hearts full of passion, jealousy and hate
woman needs man but man must have his mate
that no one can deny.
It's still the same old story, a fight for love and glory
a case of do or die.
The world will always welcome lovers as time goes by.'

'Here's looking at you, kid!'

A Sin to Tell a Lie

March 1953

She had become the Queen in June 1911 and remained so until the death of her husband, King George V, twenty five years later. But in the March of this year her heart gave out and our much respected Queen Mary passed on. Sometimes there are just a few words that tell you everything you need to know about a person; for me it was this. In one small incident in her life she demanded to see inside some slum dwellings that belonged to a charity of which she was a patron. The officials tried to dissuade her but she insisted – 'it will never be beneath my dignity to visit the homes in which my subjects have to live'. Afterwards she said – 'these houses are a disgrace to our country and an outrage upon those poor souls who live in them.' Within two months the houses had been replaced.
Perhaps like me, you still keep and cherish the Silver Jubilee medal that was issued to children in 1935.

In Kenya, Africa, there was growing unrest as an organisation called the 'Mau Mau' started violent attacks and assassinations on all levels of the population. It was the start of a series of internal conflicts that was to bring Africa to its knees over successive decades.

Looking through some newspapers of this time the following side splitting joke seemed to find great favour. We must have been easily pleased.
Old man to another old chap. 'Where be you a-going then?'
      Old chap. 'I baint a going.'
      Old man. 'Yes you be, you be a-walking.'
      Old chap. 'I baint a-going though – I'm a-coming back.'

For gardeners there was the following tip. 'Fertilise your tomatoes with a rabbit's foot. Otherwise try overhead watering.' There was no mention as to which watering device should be used for this purpose! I feel certain that ninety eight out of a hundred apprentices when asked what watering device should be used would have got the wrong answer.

May 1953

The Catholic lads had looked forward to this day. Being only a small group they had no permanent church so they accepted whatever blessings the good lord bestowed on them. Their mentor, Father Thomson, was full of enthusiasm; especially today, because today he would re-new and ignite the religious fervour of his small flock. They must not be allowed to fall by the wayside or be overwhelmed by the myriad weeds of the C of E. He had almost gone down on bended knee to persuade the authorities that something special was needed to reinforce the faith. Out of the blue had came confirmation that a coach could be booked and a place in the procession allocated. For several weeks he had, with sparkling eyes, and many a prayer, pre-blazed the trail before his khaki clad flock; the trail that led to Glastonbury and the forthcoming ascent of the Tor. With bated breath and almost overwhelmed by the sin of pride, he said they would be following in the footsteps of Joseph of Arimathea; and did not the finest hymn in England sound out the immortal words – 'and we shall build Jerusalem, in England's green and pleasant land.' As the coach pulled into the parking area Father Thomson thought his heart may burst with piety and reverential pleasure.

A Sin to Tell a Lie

Apprentice Sergeant Barlow was not so sure. Several times on the journey he had wondered if the Reverend Father was of a sound mind. Goodness knows what would be said in Yorkshire when the news filtered back! Alan Barlow had embraced the army and its traditions as he sought promotion and the protection of rank. One of the joys of promotion was the immense pleasure in delegating, especially dirty jobs, fatigues and unpleasant duties that could be heaped on the lowly. Father Thomson had seen fit to usurp his position as the senior apprentice on this church parade because he obviously considered that the delegation of duties and carrying the cross was an honoured and envied duty rather than a penance. Did he not understand that Pontius Pilate had already set the military precedent? It appeared not for the Reverend Father had babbled on. 'We lead the main procession from the old abbey to the Tor, to replicate the journey of Jesus to Calvary. Sergeant Barlow, as the senior boy - and the largest - you will have the honour of carrying the cross.'

The Sergeant had not reacted as if he was honoured; in fact his face assumed a deep frown, his eyes went a bit funny and his lips compressed. Father Thomson sensed refusal so he quickly added, "This is a great privilege, you know. It's not heavy, I had it specially made – it's a mere thirty pounds.' The journey proceeded in silence. The juniors had the sense to keep quiet, with serious faces, as they observed their Sergeant's unspoken but obvious annoyance; while Father Thomson put the quietness down to humble reverence as he silently praised God and mentally raised two fingers at the Camp Padre; albeit he was miles away.

"Everyone off the coach please and line up." Father Thomson waited as four lads carried the cross over and helped him lift it onto Sergeant Barlow's back, "There you are - light as a feather."

Sergeant Barlow blinked, he could see the Tor in the distance, "It's a long way, Father."

"No - not far – remember; we are chariots of fire today!"

"It's a blee - mountain, Father!"

"Only five hundred feet – a mere pimple, Sergeant. I am sure it will be noted in Heaven though. Everyone kneel." He put his left hand on the Sergeant's head and raised his right hand, "In nominee Patris, et Fillii, et Spiritus Sancti. The good lord will bless you son."

Sergeant Barlow braced himself as he recalled the soldiers seventh commandment – 'When you are in deep shit it is pointless asking God for help, don't forget she helped to get you there.' As they stepped out towards the Tor he was still trying to work out what he had done wrong.

THE SUMMER OF 1953.

The final six months of our three years at Beachley sped by with incredible speed. The atmosphere around us and our rising expectation was a heady mixture of fine anticipation and plain joy at being the senior group and the nearness of leaving to join the truly adult world. On Saturday mornings we drilled as a group under the RSM. He purred when we stamped in unison like the Guardsmen he would have preferred us to be and he told as stories of our heritage as soldiers. Parades and rehearsals that in previous terms had lasted for dreary hours, now passed in minutes! My trade class spent a week in Cardiff gaining practical experience of the latest electronic equipment, an analogue computer.

THE WONDERS OF DRIVING- L to R, John Jowett Rex Goddard, Jim Porter, Mr Page and Eric McDermott.

The Vehicle Mechanics were 'cock-a-hoop' taking their multiple driving tests and with each passing day we edged closer to the issue of our new uniforms and berets that preceded the final four weeks of military training, including a spell on the live firing range. From Easter onwards every week was a significant progressive event and every weekend was filled with sport and preparations for our final hours.

Many of us attended the Coronation Procession in London, just outside Buckingham Palace, as spectators on a cold and wet day – but we still raised a great cheer. On the same day came the news that Everest had been conquered and we read with pride the fact that a British Infantry Regiment had gone out in the night and decorated the enemy frontline fortifications in Korea. A few days later we paraded and presented arms while lining the route as the Queen passed by on her state visit to Cardiff.

In the last few weeks before passing out we duly duffed up RAF Cosford at athletics and cricket then a week later we tied in equal first place with RAF Halton in the inter-schools quadrangular games. Our cup overflowed!

Had we come to this time without preparation I do believe we may have failed, or at the very least collapsed from exhaustion. But no, we had spent two and a half years getting ready and we took it in our stride.

Our passing out day was fine and sunny. My parents and girlfriend arrived and after the formalities of the parade I took them around the camp, including a visit to the workshops. My

Field Marshal Harding; *'Your boys are all taller than me. Reduce the rations immediately.'*

father was most impressed with the display of electronic gadgetry while my mother was hugely impressed by the lovely uniforms and the utterly polite and deferential response she got from 'all these charming, smart and wonderful soldiers'. I tried to explain that she was a privileged visitor and they were normally quite rude and demanding. But she wouldn't have it because the army had obviously come a very long way since the Jocks destroyed Dover. I did claim and was accorded some credit for the obvious civilising effect my enlistment had had on the army and as we were related, she ultimately agreed.

In the evening I took them to dinner in the Castle Restaurant in Chepstow. Dad took one look at the menu, "Aye-op, son - it's five bob a nob! Can you afford that?"

I nodded nonchalantly, after all this was a very special day and extremely unlikely to occur again.

SCHOOL CRICKET TEAM, 1953

A Sin to Tell a Lie

March Past by 50B Group

A Sin to Tell a Lie
THE ROBOT
The following was extracted from the December 1953 copy and covers the period from **Feb 1953 to Sept 1953.**

PRIZE WINNERS 50B

Vehicle Mechanics	A Bassett, F Cresswell, J Hopwood, J Old, D Lee
Electricians	H Finnamore, M Gwinnell
Fitters	R Wooton, R Sirett, J Bacon, M Tostevin
Sheet Metal Workers	M Spinks
Education	H Finnamore, J Castell, R Rowell, R Scott
Sport	W Dallas, **Individual Athletics Cup**

SCHOOL REPRESENTATIVE COLOURS 50B

Full — W Dallas, T Sandford, P Anzalucca, B Elks, D Epps, J Harrington, M Hunt, D Long, D Lee, A Morris (Athletics). H Maisey, M McClean (Swimming). R Wooton, M Buckland, R Freeman, B Elks, R Hewton (Cricket)

FIRST CLASS CERTIFICATE OF EDUCATION 50B

A Barlow, T Boughton, E Chandler, J Green, W Green, F Hampshire, J Harris, J Hogg, J Hoit, H Johnston, E Lines, J Ripley, R Sirrett, G Tully, M Viccary, A Watford, B Willingham, R Wooton

---

NUMBERS OF QUALIFIED TRADESMEN PASSING OUT, 50B

Vehicle Mechanics	57
Electricians	19
Control Equipment Electricians	10
Fitters	32
Blacksmiths	3
Sheet Metal Workers	2
Welders	3
Total	125

A Sin to Tell a Lie
THE 50B APPRENTICES PASSING OUT LIST

TRADESMEN

The undermentioned Apprentices passed the Trade Test shown on the date stated:

Vehicle Mechanic, Group "A," Class III 13th June, 1953

22526475 D. R. Albertella
22526232 K. M. E. Andrews
22309198 P. D. Anzalucca
22526209 J. Bain
22526175 A. R. Bassett
22526230 T. Boughton
22526237 P. J. Brown
22526282 M. J. Buckland
22526159 J. F. Barlow
22526277 A. P. Castle
22526176 E. M. Chandler
22526229 R. Clough
22526164 F. Cresswell
22526292 B. S. Davis
22526275 K. Dawson
22526196 M. J. Francis
22526160 R. M. Fry
22526267 R. E. D. Gale
22526223 P. R. Giles
22526305 R. A. Goddard
22526251 J. W. Harrington
22526202 R. Hesketh
22526207 R. J. Hewton
22526216 J. M. Hopwood
22526238 T. J. Howard
22526213 J. M. Jowett
22526194 R. M. Jones
22526231 R. H. R. Kempton
22526284 C. Kennedy
22526220 D. R. Kneller
22526189 D. Lee
22526187 D. G. Lewin
22526254 W. E. Lucie
22526309 H. R. Maisey
22526243 E. J. McDermott
22526246 J. M. McKay
22526273 M. D. McLean
22309169 G. S. Ninnis
22309136 J. A. Overend
22526473 J. D. Old
22526281 T. J. A. Peacock
22526306 R. C. Poingdestre
22526165 E. J. W. Puddy
22526198 J. B. Porter
22526216 J. C. Ripley
22526157 T. E. Sanford
22526471 C. H. Simons
22526293 P. J. Sherwood
22526188 D. J. Talling
22526185 M. J. Viccary
22526173 D. Wicks
22526201 A. R. Watford
22526161 D. G. Whatley
22309199 J. R. Whitfield
22526272 E. T. F. Willingale
22526291 B. A. D. Woolsey

Engine Fitter (I.C. and Pumps), Group "A," Class III 13th June, 1953

22526256 G. T. Blower
22526274 J. A. Coomber
22526234 W. M. Green
22526257 D. Hawkeswood
22526280 L. H. Jones
22526178 F. E. Lines
22526228 E. G. W. Messer
22526255 A. C. Morris
22526250 K. Nichols
22526298 D. J. Thorndale
22526219 R. D. Wootton

Engine Fitter (I.C. and Pumps), Group "A," Class III 2nd July, 1953

22526318 M. Scott

Electrician (Vehicle and Plant), Group "A," Class III 18th June, 1953

22526167 G. S. Burgess
22526156 G. R. Church
22526183 W. C. Dallas
22526186 K. W. Down
22526182 R. H. Freeman
22526240 M. H. Gwinnell
22526210 J. H. Green
22526212 J. Harris
22526217 F. Hampshire
22526184 R. J. Harder
22526159 L. G. Johnson
22526205 B. M. Lee
22309091 D. W. Melton
22526222 C. E. Robinson
22526195 J. C. Selway
22526203 G. Stone
22526199 P. J. Sturgess
22526221 P. B. Thurgar
22526190 G. R. H. Tully

Electrician (Control Equipment) (A.A. and C.A.), Group "A," Class III, 24th June, 1953

22526233 A. E. Barlow
22526179 J. W. Castell
22526172 B. A. F. Elks
22526181 H. J. Finnamore
22526208 J. Gardner
22526192 A. R. Levitt
22526174 M. J. G. Medhurst
22526170 C. S. Montague
22526163 R. A. Rowell
22526191 R. Scott

Fitter, REME, Group "A," Class III, 13th June, 1953

22526169 M. G. Couture
22526214 B. W. A. Ennew
22526225 C. Howard
22526245 M. Hunt
22526108 P. F. Kelly
22526271 J. G. Lewis
22526249 D. Long
22526294 R. J. McDonald
22526215 P. J. Wallis
22526166 J. B. Wildish

Fitter, REME, Group "A," Class III, 18th April, 1953, and Group "A," Class II, 12th June, 1953

22526366 R. P. Sirett
22526289 M. P. Tostevin

Fitter, RE, Group "A," Class III, 13th June, 1953

22526242 J. Bacon
22526278 J. C. Collis
22526244 J. P. Durkan
22526286 D. P. Epps
22526117 T. R. Fox
22309129 J. S. Hogg
22526289 J. W. Midgley
22526285 M. J. Trivett

Blacksmith, Group "B," Class III, 13th June, 1953

22526263 D. Birchall
22526180 A. C. Booth
22526283 G. Horton

Sheet Metal Worker, Group "B," Class III 13th June, 1953

22526239 J. T. Smith
22526247 M. Spinks

Welding (Oxy-acetylene and Electric-arc), Group "B," Class III, 13th June, 1953

22526264 E. A. George
22526302 I. B. Hughes
22526197 B. R. Willingham

A Sin to Tell a Lie

Passing Out Parade

At the conclusion of the 'Passing Out' prize giving the CIGS, Field Marshall Sir John Harding said these words:-

' Remember to set your targets high. Make up your mind on this. There is a great need for craftsmen in the Army and you will be doubly welcome as regular soldiers and the skill you bring. As the professional head of the Army I welcome you most heartily and sincerely.
Remember never to stop learning and trying to excel. Enjoy your soldiering and enjoy your life.
Lastly I wish those of you who are passing out good fortune in the future – and the very best and good luck to you all.'

We were on our way,
               look out world,
                             here we come!!!

A Sin to Tell a Lie
PASSING OUT DINNER MENU

Starter

Savoury memento soup with spicy nibbles, overlaid with a garnish of old bollocks and served with 'croutons et bromide'

Main course

Roast bull glazed with an exquisite kiwi polish sauce. Served with yesterdays leftovers, seasoned with gunpowder and several overcooked vegetables. (Special Catering Corps trade test recipe). Accompanied by a glass of 'old tosh' wine.

Sweet

Upright compote of bus stop fumblings, tumbled and stirred by unfulfilled desires and swimming in memory lane sauce. Served with a crisp fan of apprentice bullshit.
Or
RSM's humble pie, served extremely rare and sprinkled with fairy tales a la cobblers.

Cheese Bored

Iron hard service biscuits served with liar's cheese and sardonic pickles.
&
River Wye Coffee and a plentiful supply of sick bags.

PS Anyone unable to listen to any more old crap about 'what we did and when' must stay and suffer until dismissed!

A Sin to Tell a Lie
PASSING OUT PARADE PROGRAMME 50B

ARMY APPRENTICES SCHOOL CHEPSTOW.

COMMANDANT - COL. W. J. SHOOLBRED. O.B.E.

PASSING OUT PARADE AND PRIZE GIVING.

23RD JULY. 1953.

REVIEWING OFFICER:

-shal SIR JOHN HARDING, G.C.B., C.B.E., D.S.O., M.C. A.D.C.

Chief of the Imperial General Staff.

Davies & Roberts Ltd., Printers, 264 High Street, Chepstow.

A Sin to Tell a Lie
PASSING OUT PARADE PROGRAMME 50B

INTRODUCTION.

To-day's Prize Giving is for apprentices who joined the School in September, 1950, 1951, and 1952.

The Parade is formed up with the Passing Out Group (50b Group), as the leading platoons of the three companies. These apprentices have completed three years of training and will now be dispersed to Corps of the Regular Army as Class III. Tradesmen. Also passing out are three R.A.M.C. apprentices, who have completed 18 months Educational and Military Training in the School and are now being posted to the R.A.M.C. Depot for advanced training.

The remainder of the Parade is composed of junior apprentices in varying stages of training. Immediately after the Parade marches off a Gymnastic Display will be given by apprentices who have been in the School for six months, and a display of advanced Physical Training by selected senior apprentices.

The Officers and N.C.O.s of the Staff do not appear on the Parade, which is under the command of the Apprentice Regimental Sergeant Major.

Apprentice i/c Parade	...	...	Apprentice R.S.M. J. D. Old.	
Incoming Apprentice R.S.M.		...	,,	C.S.M. G. F. Layton.
'B' Coy.	,,	C.S.M.	,,	C.S.M. G. R. Church.
'C' Coy.	,,	C.S.M.	,,	C.S.M. D. Lee.
'D' Coy.	,,	C.S.M.	,,	C.S.M. J. B. Wildish.

The School Band, combined with the School Corps of Drums, appears on parade, and the School Band will play for the Prize Giving. They both consist of volunteer apprentices. Sergeant J. Adams, Welch Regiment, conducts. The Apprentice Band Sergeant is Sergeant W. Green, and the Apprentice Drum Major Sergeant M. Gwinnell.

Guests are invited to visit the School Accommodation, Institutes, and Workshops in the afternoon. An Exhibition of apprentices work is displayed at the entrance to each workshop. Exhibits of the Photographic Club will be in the School Common Room.

PLAY BY SCHOOL DRAMATIC SOCIETY.

The School Amateur Dramatic Society will perform the Play "Someone at the Door," by Dorothy and Campbell Christie, in the School Theatre at 5.45 p.m. Production of the Play by Captain A. J. Lister, R.A.E.C.

A Sin to Tell a Lie
PASSING OUT PARADE PROGRAMME 50B

SEQUENCE OF THE PARADE.

10.00 a.m. - Band plays on the Parade Ground.
10.15 a.m. - Parade marches on to markers.
10.30 a.m. - The Reviewing Officer arrives and is received with a General Salute.

Inspection of the apprentices follows.

(Visitors will be seated to the right and left of the dais. As the Reviewing Officer arrives civilian guests are requested to stand. Service personnel will stand to attention but will not salute).

March past in quick time.

Presentation of the Gunnell Memorial Stick to the incoming Apprentice R.S.M.

Presentation of Long Service and Good Conduct Medal to Colour Sergeant P. Greig, The Queen's Own Cameron Highlanders.

Advance in Review Order, followed by General Salute.

Passing Out Group march off in slow time.

(Guests are requested to stand and service personnel stand to attention at this juncture).

11.15 a.m. - Physical Training Display.

In the event of wet weather the Passing Out Parade will take place in the School Gymnasium. The Outgoing Group only will be on parade. Prize Giving will follow at 11.30 a.m., also in the School Gymnasium.

PRIZE GIVING.

At 11.30 a.m. Prize Giving will take place in the School Gymnasium.

The Prayer.
Report by the Commandant.
Presentation of Prizes.
Address by the Reviewing Officer.
National Anthemn.

Lunch from 12.30—13.30, and Tea from 16.30—17.00, will be served to Parents in the School Dining Halls. Parents will be conducted to their seats for meals, and to the Play on production of the official invitation card.

A Sin to Tell a Lie
PASSING OUT PROGRAMME 50B

SCHOOL PRIZE WINNERS.

1. **WESTERN COMMAND PRIZE.** For General Excellence, with special reference to Leadership.
   Apprentice R.S.M. J. D. Old.

2. **SOUTH WALES DISTRICT PRIZE.** For General Excellence, with special reference to Educational Attainments.
   Apprentice Sjt. H. J. Finnamore.

3. **EDUCATION.**

50b Group.	51b Group.	52b Group.
Forces.	Army	Army
Preliminary Examination.	First Class Examination.	First Class Examination.
Apprentice J. W. Castell.	Apprentice L/Cpl. R. Bartrum.	Apprentice R. Wilcox.
" Sjt. H. J. Finnamore.	" R. C. Cooksley.	" T. D. Chilcott.
" R. A. Rowell.	" L/Cpl. L. J. Culverwell.	" T. C. Buttle.
" D. Scott.		" J. Darrell.
		" K. H. Bye.

   Army
   Second Class Examination.
   Apprentice Myo Sint.

4. **TRADE AND TECHNOLOGY.**

	50b Group.	51b Group.	52b Group.

   (a) *Automobile Engineering.*

First	Apprentice Cpl. A. R. Bassett.	Apprentice J. L. Fry.	Apprentice R. F. Brooker.
Second	" Sjt. F. Cresswell.	" L/Cpl. A. G. Durrant.	" G. F. H. Evans.
Third	" J. M. Hopwood.	" L/Cpl. R. J. Mullinger.	" K. W. Izzard.
Fourth	" R.S.M. J. D. Old.	" H. E. Armstrong.	" T. D. Chilcott.
Fifth	" C.S.M. D. Lee.	" G. A. Parr.	" G. E. Clements.

   (b) *Electrical Engineering.*

First	Apprentice Sjt. H. J. Finnamore.	Apprentice A. Knowles.	Apprentice G. Taylor.
Second	" Sjt. M. H. Gwinnell.	" D. J. Hill.	" E. G. Baker.
Third			" D. Mullins.

   (c) *Fitting and Machine Shop Practice.*

First	Apprentice Cpl. R. F. Sirrett.	Apprentice L/Cpl. R. Bartrum.	Apprentice A. E. Tucker.
	" R. D. Wootton.		
Second	" J. Bacon	" C. Watts.	" A. G. Fry.
	" L/Cpl. M. P. Tostevin.		

   (d) *Sheet Metal Work.*
   First   Apprentice M. Spinks.

   (e) *Blacksmith's Work.*
   First   Apprentice E. D. Sculthorpe.

   (f) *Welding Work.*
   First   Apprentice L/Cpl. G. Petty.

5. **INDIVIDUAL ATHLETES' CUP.** Presented by the Civilian Instructional Staff.
   Awarded to the apprentice adjudged to be the best all-round athlete during the preceding twelve months.
   Apprentice Cpl. W. C. Dallas.

6. INTER-COMPANY CHAMPIONSHIP HOCKEY SHIELD. 'B' Company.
7. INTER-COMPANY CHAMPIONSHIP ASSOCIATION FOOTBALL CUP. 'D' Company.
8. INTER-COMPANY CHAMPIONSHIP RUGBY FOOTBALL CUP. 'B' Company.
9. INTER-COMPANY CHAMPIONSHIP CRICKET CUP. 'C' Company.
10. INTER-COMPANY SENIOR SHOOTING CUP. 'B' Company.
11. INTER-COMPANY JUNIOR SHOOTING CUP. 'D' Company.
12. INTER-COMPANY SIX-A-SIDE HOCKEY, THE PETER TROPHY. 'D' Company.
13. INTER-COMPANY CHAMPIONSHIP SHIELD. 'D' Company.

Goodbye–e –e –e!!

Sept 1953

It is the first day of September; the day is fine, warm and sunny and there is every prospect of an 'Indian Summer'. Ronnie Marsden could sense a wonderful feeling of personal contentment about to pervade his whole being. Especially so, because he was expecting a letter that would signify freedom; a dream beautiful beyond compare. Ronnie's mind blathered on. Was it Shakespeare who had written about *'September glory fills our minds with hope for the harvest home is near, and we embrace the best time of the year'*. Captain Ronnie Marsden certainly had high hopes; his pension letter must surely be on its way. It would be nice he thought if the Government were to give the services a pay rise because the last one had been in September 1950! Never mind, he couldn't wait around for ever and he had been promised work as a 'Golf Club Secretary' to help keep the wolf from the door. The pleasurable prospect of retiring was slightly muted by the Medical Officer's opinion that he had an incipient stomach ulcer, considerable erectile malfunction, loss of bladder control and high blood pressure but Ronnie felt confident that away from the rigours of

A Sin to Tell a Lie

Beachley Camp and its pressures all would be well. He had never forgiven or forgotten the bastard who had pissed in his carafe - whoever he was! He was convinced it was that episode which had caused his ulcer. Since that day he had never been able to view the carafe in the same affectionate way because of that disgusting abuse but all that was behind him now. Drifting into the distant past.

The last possible culprits who could have violated his carafe had been marched to the buses four days ago. May whoever it was rest in hell, he thought. The president of the officers' mess had enquired of his view about a retirement dinner and he felt confident that a small token of esteem would be presented. He stared at the nice cut glass tumbler on his desk, engraved 'Champion Company 1950'. That had been his award in July 1950 when C Company had been declared as the 'Champion Company'. Gammy Peter, the old colonel, had said 'well done Ronnie' when he handed it over. Ronnie had smiled a 'thank you, sir', despite the fact that his transfer request had been binned unceremoniously. Now, where had he put his carafe? It should have been up on the shelf where it had rested for two years. Naturally he didn't look at it every day, but certainly it had been there two days ago, of that he was sure. Never mind, the Sar'nt Major would know. There was a knock on the door and Sergeant Swift put his head round the door. "Just putting the kettle on, Sir, thought you may like a cuppa."

"Thank you, the usual please."

A hand went out smartly. "That will be two shillings, Sir, you forgot to pay last week." And you're not getting away with it again, you crafty bastard!

The two shillings was handed over in silence. "Has the mail arrived yet, Sergeant?"

"Just arrived, Sir, the Sar'nt Major will be with you in two minutes."

A Sin to Tell a Lie

Dead on time CSM Kidd knocked and entered. "The list of the new lads has come, Sir." The usual transfer from H.Q. Company was due tomorrow. "I've given the 'Q' the details."

Captain Marsden drummed his fingers in frustration, "Apprentices, Sar'nt Major, apprentices."

"Yes, sorry, Sir; apprentices it is. There's a small package for you, Sir. Marked private. I don't think it can be your pension letter." He smiled to diminish the blow. "Better luck tomorrow."

The Captain frowned, was no piece of private information secret in this damn camp. Bloody hell, the Colonel had only got to fart, or use more than one 'french letter' a quarter, and everyone knew within seconds - and now his pension letter was going the rounds!

"Have you seen my carafe, Sar'nt Major?"

"No Sir." He looked up to the shelf, squinting with effort, "It was on the shelf - oh, I see what you mean, Sir, its gone!"

Ronnie picked up the small package, wondering idly what it could be, "Have a look around the offices. It can't be far."

"Right you are, Sir." The door closed

Ronnie opened the package, it was rather poorly wrapped. As he unfolded the contents a key dropped onto his desk. The paper around the key was obviously a note, though rather crumpled. He smoothed it out and read.

'CAPTAIN MARSDEN BASTURD, I HAVE RETURNED YOUR KEY. I DID NOT GET IN THE WINDOW I ONLY TOOK OUT THE PUTTY AND LOOSENNED THE GLASS TO MAKE IT LOKE AS IF I DID. I FOUND THE KEY TO THE OFFICE DOOR THE DAY BEFORE. AS YOU WERE A NASTY BASTARD I PISSED IN YOUR JAR COS YOU HAD PISSED ME OFF BY THE TIME YOU GET THIS LETTER I SHALL BE LONG GONE I WILL NEVER FORGIT YOU I USED THE KEY FOR THE LAS T TIME THE OTHER NIGHT.

A Sin to Tell a Lie

I HAD BEEN OUT WIV A GIRL AND CUMBED THREE TIMES IN MY PANTS. I WIPED YOUR GLASS WIV MY PANTS AND I TIYED THE PANTS AROUND YOUR JAR WHITCH IS IN THE FILING CABENET. I HOPE YOU NEVER FORGIT ME. THE PISS ARTIST of 50B'

For a few exhilarating moments Ronnie's hopes could have scaled a mountain as he considered a formal complaint and the arrival of the Military Police Special Branch. He would demand that they fingerprint the entire bloody group to identify the culprit; but that thought was quickly squashed. Even if the culprit was charged and sentenced it would still make him into a laughing stock. He repeated the word 'bastard' several times as he took out his lighter and burnt the letter, before he subsided in frustration. Oh God, the bastard had used his underpants to clean my glass! He desperately tried to recall how many times he had used it over the last few days! "Sar'nt Major!"

CSM Kidd hurried in, "Yes Sir." He sniffed, "No trouble I hope, sir?"

"Open that cabinet, please. See if my carafe is in there."

The drawers rattled back, one by one, "Ah - here it is, Sir."

"Thank you - put it in the rubbish bin. And this glass as well."

"Right this minute, Sir?"

"Immediately."

He held out the carafe. "It has a pair of khaki pants tied to it, Sir. Do you want them retrieved?" He wondered if the C.O. had been drinking again, his eyes searched the room for evidence of a bottle. He was about to say 'And that's your champion company glass, sir' but wasn't quick enough.

The fast reply was more a growl than anything. "Certainly not, Sar'nt Major – and if I hear one whisper of this on the bush telegraph I shall make your life a fuckin' misery during my last few days here."

A Sin to Tell a Lie

"You mustn't get upset, Sir. Think of your ulcer and your heart."

Ronnie's hand went to his head in despair as he closed his eyes in frustration. 'Oh, God, is my medical condition being discussed by all and sundry.'

CSM Kidd unwittingly set a match to the oil already spilt on troubled waters. "I'm sure it's only someone taking the piss, Sir. I expect it's just an old cleaning rag one of the lads left lying around. Nothing to really worry about. We must concentrate on being Champion Company once more."

"I shall be long gone, I hope."

"Old soldiers never die, as they say, sir. Which reminds me, the RQMS wants a squad of lads to get the rooms ready for the Old Boys Reunion."

Ronnie closed his eyes, bollocks to the Beachley Old Boys. "Give the Orderly Room a call and ask your mate, the Chief Clerk, if he can chase up my pension letter will you."

CSM Kidd clicked his heels, "Already done, Sir." As fuckin' always he thought as he left. Then his face brightened as he remembered that Mrs Kidd sometimes demanded a good rogering on a Friday evening after Bingo. Perhaps this was his lucky day. He started to whistle as he went back to the office. Sergeant Swift looked at him. "What are you doing with those, Harry?"

The CSM inclined his head, "He wants'em thrown out!"

Speedy pointed to his head, "I don't think it's just his blood pressure, ulcer and cock that have gone wrong. Too much time bending over for the Colonel I reckon. There's ambition for you, he should have learnt the trumpet."

"Did you hear that Busty Baker is going soon?"

"I don't believe it! Where are they going to find civvies large enough for him?"

"I heard tell that the RAF is donating a barrage balloon!"

"They'll need two! And that's no lie."

A Sin to Tell a Lie

The telephone rang, Speedy answered. "Yes, Sar'nt Major------right-------------Oh dear----------------right away-------of course------I understand."

CSM Kidd frowned, "What the hell was that all about?"

"That was the RSM. Apparently there are several policemen on their way here with a warrant to arrest the CQMS. Something about a dodgy accumulator bet – he reckons Colonel Shoolbred is as mad as a hatter and wants to see the CO at once."

"Bloody hell! This is not going to do his ulcer any good."

"Fuck his ulcer! Are you any good at lying?"

"Why?"

"I wrote out our weekend bets an' took'em round to the store, twenty minutes ago."

"Oh, shit!"

The Colonel's eyes narrowed as he inspected Captain Marsden. "How did this happen?" His tone of voice was critical.

"I have no idea, Sir." It was said optimistically in the hope of deflecting a detailed dissection of his leadership skills.

"No idea! Right under your nose one of your NCO's commits fraud and you say 'I have no idea'."

"I'm sure it wasn't done in the camp, Sir and I cannot oversee his private life."

"Don't be facetious! Soldiers have no private life. This disgraceful behaviour will affect our reputation and my standing at the golf club. Besides which I'm told that this NCO was running a betting shop within yards of your office!"

Behind his back, Ronnie crossed his fingers and blessed CSM Kidd and Sergeant Swift; they had emptied the company storeroom of any evidence in minutes. The incriminating betting slips and lists had already been safely destroyed. "I cannot believe McCloud was using camp facilities, Sir. In fact I am absolutely certain of it. It is possible that the CQMS fooled

A Sin to Tell a Lie

us. He is, I believe, an accomplished liar. The army will be better off without him I'm sure, should he prove to be guilty."

The Colonel did not look convinced, "You only have a few more days with us, try to ensure that everything is under control. It would be a pity to end a career under a cloud." He stopped and smiled, "I say, that's rather good, eh? Under a Mc—Cloud." He gave a constrained brief chuckle but Ronnie remained pow-faced so the Colonel continued, "Your successor arrives early next week; get ready to hand over then. Show him the ropes; make him feel at home, eh! I know you've enjoyed your time here so fire him up. There's a good chap."

"Naturally, Sir, it will be my pleasure. I've loved every minute here." Suddenly the future seemed brighter as a thought crossed his mind. *Perhaps this new fella would like a rather nice carafe and glass for his desk, so he'll feel at home.*

CSM Kidd looked across at Sergeant Swift, "That was a bloody close call, Speedy."

"Too close for my liking, Harry. That could have been the jolly old pension down the plughole!"

"Have you never thought of writing a song? You could make a fortune with your musical talent."

Speedy looked pensive, a nostalgic note in his voice, "I did write a song once- a bloody good one too."

CSM Kidd's eyebrows lifted in expectation, "Well – what happened to it?"

"I sent it to the publishers. They said the melody was absolutely fantastic but the title was much too long." His face was really sad as he spoke, even sadder than his voice.

"Oh! What was it called?"

"Whenever I Dream of You, My Darling Lovely Sweetheart of a Sergeant Major, I Get Such a Bleedin' Great Hard On!"

"I love you too - you---!"

A Sin to Tell a Lie

*'Be sure it's true when you say I love you,
                 it's a sin to tell a lie
Millions of hearts have been broken,
           just because these words were spoken.
   I love you, I love you
                        --- I love you............'*

MORE MEMENTOES

OF

BEACHLEY DAYS

'YOU'LL NEVER FORGET ME – I'M GONNA BE LIKE A FARVER AN' A MUVVER TO YER!!!!!'

232

A Sin to Tell a Lie
PASSING OUT SEVICE

ARMY APPRENTICES SCHOOL
BEACHLEY.

✝

50b PASSING OUT SERVICE

SUNDAY, 23RD AUGUST, 1953

School Chapel,
Beachley.

A Sin to Tell a Lie
PASSING OUT SERVICE

Order of Service.

PRAISE to the Lord, the Almighty, the King of creation;
O my soul, praise him, for he is thy health and salvation:
All ye who hear, now to his temple draw near,
Joining in glad adoration.

Praise to the Lord, who o'er all things so wondrously reigneth,
Shieldeth thee gently from harm, or when fainting sustaineth:
Hast thou not seen how thy heart's wishes have been
Granted in what he ordaineth.

Praise to the Lord, who doth prosper thy work and defend thee;
Surely his goodness and mercy shall daily attend thee:
Ponder anew what the Almighty can do,
If to the end he befriend thee.

Praise to the Lord! O let all that is in me adore him!
All that hath life and breath, come now with praises before him!
Let the Amen sound from his people again:
Gladly for aye we adore him.

CEREMONY OF THE NAMES.

The Chaplain: They that wait upon the Lord shall renew their strength, they shall mount up with wings as eagles; they shall run and not be weary; they shall walk and not faint.

Brethren, we have come together in the presence of Almighty God to offer to Him our praises and our thanksgiving for all the benefits we have received at his hands: to pray for grace and strength to live our lives according to his holy will and to dedicate ourselves to his service, that we may prove worthy to be the leaders and servants of those with whom we are called upon to serve. Let us, therefore, kneel in silence and remember God's presence with us now.

THE SILENCE.
THE LORD'S PRAYER.
PSALM 15.

Lord, who shall dwell in thy tabernacle: or who shall rest upon thy holy hill?

Even he, that leadeth an uncorrupt life: and doeth the thing which is right, and speaketh the truth from his heart.

He that hath used no deceit in his tongue, nor done evil to his neighbour: and hath not slandered his neighbour.

He that setteth not by himself, but is lowly in his own eyes: and maketh much of them that fear the Lord.

He that sweareth unto his neighbour, and disappointeth him not: though it were to his own hindrance.

He that hath not given his money upon usury; nor taken reward against the innocent.

Whoso doeth these things: shall never fall.

Glory be to the Father, and to the Son: and to the Holy Ghost; As it was in the beginning, is now and ever shall be: world without end. Amen.

A Sin to Tell a Lie
PASSING OUT SERVICE

THE FIRST LESSON.   THE COMMANDANT.
ISAIAH 40, 25-31.

Guide me, O thou great Redeemer,
   Pilgrim through this barren land;
I am weak, but thou art mighty;
Hold me in thy powerful hand;
   Bread of heaven,
Feed me now and evermore.

Open now the crystal fountain
Whence the healing stream doth flow;
Let the fiery cloudy pillar
Lead me all my journey through:
   Strong deliverer,
Be thou still my strength and shield.

When I tread the verge of Jordan,
Bid my anxious fears subside;
Death of death, and hell's destruction,
Land me safe on Canaan's side:
   Songs and praises
I will ever give to thee.

THE SECOND LESSON.   Apprentice Sergeant E. McDERMOTT.
ST. MATTHEW 20, 20-28.

He who would valiant be
   'Gainst all disaster,
Let him in constancy
Follow the Master.
There's no discouragement
Shall make him once relent
His first avowed intent
   To be a pilgrim.

Who so beset him round
   With dismal stories,
Do but themselves confound—
   His strength the more is.
No foes shall stay his might,
Though he with giants fight:
He will make good his right
   To be a pilgrim.

Since, Lord, thou dost defend
   Us with thy Spirit,
We know we at the end
   Shall life inherit.
Then fancies flee away!
I'll fear not what men say
I'll labour night and day
   To be a pilgrim.

THE THIRD LESSON.   Apprentice R.S.M. J. OLD.
II CORINTHIANS 4, 1-7.

THE PRAYERS.

And did those feet in ancient time
   Walk upon England's mountains green?
And was the Holy Lamb of God
   On England's pleasant pastures seen?
And did the Countenance Divine
   Shine forth upon our clouded Hills?
And was Jerusalem builded here
   Among those dark Satanic mills?

A Sin to Tell a Lie
PASSING OUT SERVICE

    Bring me my bow of burning gold!
      Bring me my arrows of desire!
    Bring me my spear! O clouds unfold!
      Bring me my Chariot of Fire!
    I will not cease from mental fight;
      Nor shall my sword sleep in my hand
    Till we have built Jerusalem
      In England's green and pleasant land.

THE ADDRESS.

LAND of our birth, we pledge to thee
    Our love and toil in the years to be;
When we are grown and take our place,
As men and women with our race.

Father in Heaven who lovest all,
O help thy children when they call,
That they may build from age to age
An undefiled heritage.

Teach us to bear the yoke in youth,
With steadfastness and careful truth;
That, in our time thy grace may give
The truth whereby the nations live.

Teach us to rule ourselves alway
Controlled and cleanly night and day;
That we may bring, if need arise,
No maimed or worthless sacrifice.

Teach us to look in all our ends
On thee for judge, and not our friends;
That we, with thee, may walk uncowed
By fear or favour of the crowd.

Teach us the strength that cannot seek
By deed or thought, to hurt the weak;
That, under thee, we may possess
Man's strength to comfort man's distress.

Teach us delight in simple things,
And mirth that has no bitter springs;
Forgiveness free of evil done,
And love to all men 'neath the sun.

Land of our birth, our faith, our pride,
For whose dear sake our fathers died;
O Motherland, we pledge to thee,
Head, heart and hand through the years
                      to be.

THE NATIONAL ANTHEM.
THE BLESSING.

After which all will remain kneeling while the following is sung:

    God be in my head, And in my understanding;
    God be in my eyes, And in my looking;
    God be in my mouth, And in my speaking;
    God be in my heart, And in my thinking;
    God be at mine end, And at my departing.

A Sin to Tell a Lie
APPRENTICESHIP CERTIFICATE

22309221

ARMY APPRENTICES SCHOOL
CHEPSTOW

This is to Certify that Apprentice Tradesman Serjeant

JOSEPH ALFRED P. KINSON

undertook an Engineering Apprenticeship

from 6th February, 1950 to 5th February, 1953 on completion of which he obtained the following grading :

FITTER, Class III.

He also gained some experience in the allied trades and subjects of :

MACHINE SHOP PRACTICE.
AUTOMOBILE ENGINEERING.
ELECTRICAL WORK.
SMITHING AND WELDING.

The following additional qualifications were obtained :

ARMY SECOND CLASS CERTIFICATE OF EDUCATION.
ARMY FIRST CLASS CERTIFICATE OF EDUCATION.

During his training at this School his conduct was Excellent.

Dated 5th February, 1953.

Colonel,
Commandant
Army Apprentices School

A Sin to Tell a Lie
APPRENTICESHIP CERTIFICATE

ARMY APPRENTICES SCHOOL

This is to Certify that Apprentice Tradesman Lance-Corporal

BRIAN ALBERT F. PLES

undertook an Engineering Apprenticeship

from 4th September, 1950 to 28th August, 1953 on completion of which he obtained the following grading :

ELECTRICIAN, Class III.

He also gained some experience in the allied trades and subjects of :

FITTING AND MACHINE SHOP PRACTICE.

SHEET METAL WORK.

The following additional qualifications were obtained :

ARMY SECOND CLASS CERTIFICATE OF EDUCATION.
ARMY FIRST CLASS CERTIFICATE OF EDUCATION.
English, Mathematics, General Knowledge and Part II
of
FORCES PRELIMINARY CERTIFICATE OF EDUCATION.

During his training at this School his conduct was Very Good.
Awarded Representative School Colour
for
ATHLETICS and CRICKET.

Dated 28th August, 1953.

Colonel,
Commandant
Army Apprentices School

A Sin to Tell a Lie
EDUCATION CERTIFICATE

7067
Army Form C. 313

ARMY CERTIFICATE OF EDUCATION

FIRST CLASS

This is to certify that at an examination held under the authority of the Army Council 2 2 A/T Brian Albert Frederick ELKS satisfied the examiners in

PART I: ENGLISH, MATHEMATICS, CURRENT AFFAIRS

PART II: GENERAL SCIENCE, APPLIED MAP READING

TO TAKE EFFECT FROM 20th March, 1952

Colonel.
COMMANDANT, INSTITUTE OF ARMY EDUCATION.

DIRECTOR OF ARMY EDUCATION.

A Sin to Tell a Lie
ACKNOWLEDGEMENT

In the preparation of this book I was kindly allowed access to the Beachley Old Boys Association's archive that is preserved at Beachley and looked after by a dedicated Committee of ex-apprentices so that our heritage can be passed down to posterity. This work is additional to all the time and effort needed to organise and run the Association. The Committee deserves our thanks and appreciation; they also deserve our whole hearted support. No doubt the work load will increase as word of the existence of the Association spreads. New BOBA is self funding and each year organises a reunion weekend, a source of great pleasure and comradeship. Also a magazine is produced so we can keep in touch with what is happening and I find myself invariably turning to the page of 'new members' before anything else to see who has turned up – I am rarely disappointed.
My special thanks must go to John Furley, Malcolm Hay and Joe Kinson for their help in passing on to me precious lists, documents and photographs from our Beachley days for incorporation with the text. But I must not forget those old comrades who rallied around with reminders, anecdotes, mementoes and memories.

Those who watch the November Remembrance Service on TV on Armistice Sunday must surely have felt a stir of pride as the Beachley Boys have marched past the Cenotaph in recent years. Also I have been greatly impressed by the pride, standards, skill and attitude of the modern day army. I would like to think that we made our contribution to the ongoing legacy of professional pride that I have observed in what are extremely difficult and hazardous circumstances.

A Sin to Tell a Lie

Looking back to my own time at Beachley I feel it is only fair to mention the dedication of the many members of staff who looked after us. They rarely worked nine to five! Often it was more like eight am to nine pm, including weekends!! The playing fields of Beachley were a wonderful ground for development, both for skill and character. I trust that I will be forgiven for the attempt at humour in this book; sincerely it is not meant, nor ever meant, to belittle people or make them seem merely foolish. But rather to make them human and provoke smiles rather than tears. The funny side of army service often sustained us in the difficult times; despair never ruled our lives. *(For many years I had a German friend and she said it was the British penchant for humour that won the war and sustained us through the darkest days. If only we didn't throw litter about we would be the perfect people!)* At Beachley we embraced the humour alongside the team spirit and learnt to march with pride, some even into old age. I think also we learnt that the army is truly based upon only one attribute, one theme and one constant – comradeship.

Can you hear the Band playing – the marching steps – the crowded streets by the Cenotaph? Some of the marchers may be getting older but you see the backs straighten and the heads lift up. Surely you can see them! Our yesterdays, our today and our tomorrows. Sing along now –

'Pack up your troubles in your old kit bag
And smile, smile, smile
While you've a Lucifer to light your fag
Smile boys that's the style
What's the use of worrying – it never was worthwhile
So pack up your troubles in your old kit bag
And smile, smile, smile………………………....'

A Sin to Tell a Lie
THE INITIAL ROLL CALL (Feb 1950)

50A Group

Robert S Sandall
Peter M Baugh
Arthur R Piti-Pladdy
Alan E Skinner
Donald A Jacobs
Derek W Melton
Anthony J Webb
Michael A Beresford
Peter D Smith
John S Hogg
Arthur B Rhodes
Harvey Barker
James A Neilson
Cecil W Black
Albert F Weyman
John Hoyle
Arnold J Overd
William A Graves
Roy E Wells
Brian Rowson
Brian Elliot
Henry E Williams
Richard C Hyde
Roy K Barnett
John H Cox
Michael B Allen
Terry J Denton
Peter D Phillips
Gerald S Ninnis
Alan E Appleton

Wilfred Sawyer
Francis C English
Leslie Drury
David O Moss
Terence D Ingles
Daniel J Leach
Richard Taylor

Robert H Foster
James H Harris
Jacques R Hardy
James A Overend
Roy A Smith
John B Brennan
Terence M Gleeson
John H Moore
Frederick G Dale
Anthony Morris
Brian Banyard
Bernard E Bull
Ronald J Overd
Thomas Jennings
Peter R Herrett
Donald A Curtis
Geoffrey P Pendle
William A Dewar
Peter D Denton
Terrence L Price
Donald F Moran
Frank Butler

A Sin to Tell a Lie
THE INITIAL ROLL CALL (Feb 1950)

50A Group

Francis Sperring	Keith Walton
Arthur Fowler	John T Bright
Anthony Millburn	John C Marshall
William E Flude	Frederick C Mortimer
Reginald Day	David R Leswell
John M Whelan	Colin W Williams
Irving Chew	Kenneth Trowsdale
Donald Morrison	Ian R Rumble
Alexander D Burden	Arthur W Milton
Robert T Bindloss	Gordon G Robinson
Alan G Vosper	Peter A Bignall
Alan Turner	Patrick D Anzalucca
John R Whitfield	Frank S Goddard
Colin Squire	Richard S Fahey
Malcolm Bradbury	David W Boycott
David Bevan	Michael J Matthews
Brian K Taylor	Rodney Commins
Leslie M Porter	Colin H Bibb
James Kearns	Raymond Winter
Francis G Davidson	Anthony Theobald
Ean J Wood	Joseph A Kinson
Victor G Church	Ronald J Wright
Nicholas A Winter	Michael J Kimber

A Sin to Tell a Lie
THE INITIAL ROLL CALL (Sept 1950)

50B Group

Greatorex R Church	Herbert M Latimer
James B Wildish	Patrick H Leader
Brian A Elks	Arthur R Bassett
John W Castell	Brian R Willingham
Michael J Medhurst	Anthony R Watford
Ronald Hesketh	Charles A Garrett
John Gardner	John Harris
Charles E Robinson	Peter R Giles
Christopher Howard	Terence Boughton
Malcolm H Gwinnell	Robert A Unwin
Dennis Long	George T Blower
Allen P Castle	Graham E Gillman
Thomas J Peacock	Michael J Buckland
Donald P Epps	Basil L Wilkins
Reginald C Poingdestre	Walter M Green
Malcom M Roberts	Thomas E Sandford
Peter E Kelly	Rodney M Fry
Frank Cresswell	Robert H Freeman
Michael J Viccary	Kenneth W Down
Alan R Levitt	Henry Johnston
Martin J Francis	Timothy E Quinlan
Ian G Johnson	Dennis Birchall
Arthur E George	Robert E Gale
John W Bowers	George Horton
Michael J Trivett	Roy Higham
Anthony J Howard	Raymond J McDonald
Daniel J Thorndale	Duncan Elsworth
David W Cowlard	John D Old
Raymond K Wort	John M Hopwood
Keith M Andrews	Alan E Barlow

A Sin to Tell a Lie
THE INITIAL ROLL CALL (Sept 1950)

50B Group

John P Durkan
James V Gethin
Malcolm D McClean
John C Collis
Michael P Tostevin
Alan McCormack
John Bacon
Eric J McDermott
Melvin S Davies
Clive S Montague
William C Dallas
George R Tully
John Bain
John C Ripley
Peter B Thurgar
Jack A Coomber
Bernard S Davis
John F Barlow
David J Talling
David G Lewin
John C Selway
Basil W Ennew
Frank Hampshire
Michael Scott
John A Hoit
Roy H Kemp
John T Smith
John M McKay
William E Lucie
Richard G Carlton

Kenneth Nichols
Robert Lochrie
Keith Dawson
Charles Kennedy
Ivor B Hughes
William R Pugh
Leonard C Clements
Michael Spinks
Geoffrey S Burgess
Harold J Finnamore
Anthony Allen
George Stone
John M Jowett
Raymond D Wooton
Peter J Brown
Brian A Woolsey
Clive H Simons
Roy A Rowell
Michael G Couture
Ronald M Jones
Peter J Sturgess
Peter J Wallis
Paul Peters
David R Kneller
Edward G Messer
Terence J Howard
Michael Hunt
John W Harrington
Raymond G Laming
Frederick J Sherwood

A Sin to Tell a Lie
THE INITIAL ROLL CALL (Sept 1950)

50B

Dennis R Albertella	John E Ransom
Edward J Puddy	Donald Wicks
Thomas R Fox	Ronald Scott
James B Porter	Brian M Lee
Robert J Hewton	John H Green
Roy Clough	Ian G Middleton
Albert C Morris	Derek Hawkswood
Roy F Sirett	John W Midgley
James G Lewis	Edward T Willingale
Barrie A Smith	Robert J Rippey
Lyndon H Jones	Alfred C Mathlin
William J Donald	Howard R Maisey
Francis Smith	Donald G Whatley
Eric M Chandler	Frank E Lines
Anthony C Booth	Donald Lee
Allan MacInnes	Robert J Harder

Out of the total of 257 boys who enlisted in 1950 some 42 of them (just over 16%) did not make it to Passing Out Day.

These lists are produced in the order in which they appear in the School Record Book, hence the alphabetic irregularity. The size difference between the A and B groups was a normal pattern repeated over the years.

A Sin to Tell a Lie
ONCE THEY WERE BOYS!

Near the beginning I said we did not want to grow old because there is still so much to achieve. Also there is scientific progress! Let's face it; if Viagra works maybe science will find the solution to fading memories, baldness, fallen arches and stop hair growing out of our ears! On yer knees, lads and put your hands together in prayer.

COMMANDMENTS FOR SOLDIERS

1. The Army is not God; when this change occurs it will appear on Part 1 Orders.
2. Love the Army with all your might but do not expect any Valentines.
3. Do not get caught but if you are first deny, then lie otherwise plead insanity.
4. When you hear a voice inviting volunteers run like hell.
5. Never inform on a comrade.
6. Any person of whatever rank who wears a long service and good conduct medal deserves your admiration because they haven't been caught yet.
7. When you are up to your bollocks in shit do not ask God for help, remember, She helped to guide you there.
8. Do not piss-off your superior whilst they can retaliate.
9. Never use one swear word when several will get the job done properly.
10. The application or over-use of bullshit simply means you are an arsehole.

'I SO SWEAR THAT THROUGHOUT THIS BOOK I HAVE TOLD THE TRUTH, THE WHOLE TRUTH AND NOTHING BUT THE TRUTH........EXCEPT WHEN I HAVE LIED.'

A Sin to Tell a Lie
SOME FINAL THOUGHTS

The following two poems were written before this book was thought about. The passing away of old friends has always been painful. In recent years this has unfortunately become more frequent. There is a terrible poignancy in being told that an old friend, even someone you had almost forgotten, was no longer here and you wish you had kept in touch more often. Also there was the peculiar shock some years ago to discover that the old school was no longer there! Who dare destroy our memories– who dare to take away our youth? But then time passes. It made me think because one day inevitably there will only be one Beachley Boy left and I wondered what he might say in farewell.

OLD FRIENDS PASSING BY
Should I feel heartache as old friends pass on by
  How else, for they will all be greatly missed.
Should I feel anger as old friends pass me by
  And leave me here to mourn their passing.
Must I lament as old friends pass on by
  When my memory is filled with smiling faces.

Shall I weep as old friends walk on by
  When it is their laughter fills my thoughts.
For did not they live lives so very rich
  With courage, humour and such joyful hope.
So should I feel sorrow as they pass on by?
  No they would not ask for sorrow or regret.

No weeping, anger, lamentation would they want
  What use are those when you must celebrate a life.
I am in mourning as old friends pass me by,
  Dressed in black to mark the day but in my heart
It is the courage, humour and the joyful hope
  That reigns and will sustain me to the end.

THE LAST BEACHLEY BOY

We stood together youthful comrades all, bound fast to each other by an esprit fiercely held. Great sporting battles we did hold, and stood in line abreast and proud as any British Guards.

Now I look back on all the years of loyal service but alas for some there was no long life, they lost it in their prime. But the memories cannot fade for me as my advancing years make the memories of the good days of our youth grow stronger. Those far off days when we were full of hope and the future held no fear, just the glory of living side by side, bonded as brothers.

But those bright lads now have gone forever and although I see them plain, my heart can hold no joy, for I am upstanding with my glass in hand and my head unbowed in service to my country and all my friends.
I am the last Beachley Boy.

CHEERS!

Thank you all for all the memories.

A Sin to Tell a Lie
Best Joke I Remember during my Service Time

A German officer was demonstrating the art of drill to his military students with the aid of a platoon of trained ants. Backwards and forward the ants marched; left turn, right turn, about turn. All in perfect precision in accordance with the words of command; because these were German Ants. At last he halted them and they stood motionless, waiting for the next order.

"Vell, vot do you sink of zem?"

"Ve are all astounded," said one student, "but ve are puzzled. How do zese ants hear you, mien instructor, zey have no ears?"

"Javol! Very astute. Zey hear me through zee legs. I vill demonstrate."

He picked up an ant and carefully pulled off all its legs and dropped it back in position. "Now votch!" He then gave the order to quick march and all the ants marched forward except the ant with no legs. "Zere! You see, he cannot hear me."

"How do ve know you are right, mien instructor?" ventured a student.

"You disbelieve me! I vont you all to picks up zis ant and inspect it carefully for ears."

One by one the students picked up the ant and studied it. No, no ears. One by one they dropped it back into place until the last student who picked it up and looked at it, said. "Herr Instructor, zis poor ant is crying. I can see tears in its eyes."

"Vot did you expect you dumbkof, I did not zay he felt no pain. Zese ants are not zee tough British Tommies ve fight who vould laugh at such treatment, mien gott! After all, zis poor German ant has been dropped from a great height onto his bollocks twelve times!"

Sorry about that but you must have realised by this page that I'm a sad case, BE.

A Sin to Tell a Lie

The Author with the CEO of Hewlett Packard in 1990 when I was invited to launch their latest commercial disc drive. I include this only as evidence that I had, by that time, nearly learnt how to stand properly 'at ease'! I feel certain that dear Sergeant Emery would have been proud of me, God bless him.

A Sin to Tell a Lie
Post Beachley. September 1953 to June 1957.

National Certificate in Electrical Engineering
Awarded jointly by The Institution of Electrical Engineers and the Ministry of Education

ORDINARY GRADE

This is to certify that

BRIAN ALBERT FREDERICK KLEE

has completed an approved PART-TIME COURSE in ELECTRICAL ENGINEERING at TECHNICAL INSTITUTE, ASHFORD

and has satisfied the Assessors appointed by The Institution of Electrical Engineers in the Examination in the Final Year—

SUBJECTS OF THE COURSE

First Year
    Engineering Drawing
    (Exempted from: Practical Mathematics;
    Engineering Science)

Second Year
    Electrical Engineering
    Engineering Science
    Practical Mathematics

Final Year
    Practical Mathematics
    Electrical Engineering (A.C.)
    Electrical Engineering (D.C.)

Secretary of The Institution of Electrical Engineers

Under Secretary of the Ministry of Education

Dated this day of August 19 55

Principal of Technical Institute, Ashford

Conditions governing the award of this Certificate are printed on the back

For three years from 1953 to 1956, after Beachley, I worked alongside John Finnamore in the AA Command School of Technical Instruction at Lydd, Kent. In 1955 we both gained an ONC at Ashford Technical College.

A Sin to Tell a Lie
Post Beachley

National Certificate in Electrical Engineering
Awarded jointly by The Institution of Electrical Engineers and the Ministry of Education

ORDINARY GRADE

This is to certify that

JOHN HAROLD FINNAMORE

has completed an approved PART-TIME COURSE in ELECTRICAL ENGINEERING at TECHNICAL INSTITUTE, ASHFORD

and has satisfied the Assessors appointed by The Institution of Electrical Engineers in the Examination in the Final Year

SUBJECTS OF THE COURSE

First Year
 Engineering Drawing
 (Exempted from Practical Mathematics)
 Engineering Science

Second Year
 Electrical Engineering
 Engineering Science
 Practical Mathematics

Final Year
 Practical Mathematics
 Electrical Engineering (A.C.) – with Distinction
 Electrical Engineering (D.C.) – with Distinction

Secretary of The Institution of Electrical Engineers

Under Secretary of the Ministry of Education

Dated this 24th day of August 19 55

Principal of Technical Institute, Ashford.

Conditions governing the award of this Certificate are printed on the back.

A further year at Canterbury Technical College put us within striking distance of an HNC but our close association ended with the demise of AA Command.

A Sin to Tell a Lie
Post Beachley

National Certificate in Electrical Engineering
Awarded jointly by The Institution of Electrical Engineers and the Ministry of Education

HIGHER GRADE

This is to certify that

JOHN HAROLD FITZGERALD

has completed an approved PART-TIME COURSE in ELECTRICAL ENGINEERING at CENTRAL TECHNICAL COLLEGE, EXETER

and has satisfied the Assessors appointed by The Institution of Electrical Engineers in the Examination in the Final Year

SUBJECTS OF THE COURSE

First Year
- Practical Mathematics
- Electrical Machinery
- Electrical Technology

Final Year
- Applied Mechanics
- Practical Mathematics
- Electrical Technology
- Distribution and Utilisation

Secretary of The Institution of Electrical Engineers

Under Secretary of the Ministry of Education

Dated this 19th day of September, 19 57

Principal of Central Technical College, Exeter

Conditions governing the award of this Certificate are printed on the back

John went on to 2nd Training Battalion and finished his HNC at Exeter Central Technical College in 1957.

A Sin to Tell a Lie
Beachley again!

National Certificate in Electrical Engineering
Awarded jointly by The Institution of Electrical Engineers and the Ministry of Education

HIGHER GRADE

This is to certify that

_____

has completed an approved PART-TIME COURSE in ELECTRICAL ENGINEERING at Newport Technical College, Monmouthshire

and has satisfied the Assessors appointed by The Institution of Electrical Engineers in the Examination in the Final Year

SUBJECTS OF THE COURSE

First Year
- Mathematics
- Electrical Power
- Electrical Technology

Final Year
- Electrical Power
- Applied Mechanics
- Electrical Engineering – with Distinction

Secretary of The Institution of Electrical Engineers

Permanent Secretary of the Welsh Department of the Ministry of Education

Dated this 7th day of June, 1957

Principal of Newport Technical College, Monmouthshire

Conditions governing the award of this Certificate are printed on the back

I returned to Beachley and finished my HNC at Newport Technical College in June 1957. We were, I believe, the first Beachley Boys to complete this technical hurdle within this time frame straight after leaving. Believe me when I say that I had never worked so hard in all my life!

A Sin to Tell a Lie
Personal Notes & Photos

A Sin to Tell a Lie

Personal Notes & Photos

A Sin to Tell a Lie
Personal Notes & Photos

A Sin to Tell a Lie

Personal Notes & Photos